Woman, Thou Art Loosed!

DEVOTIONAL

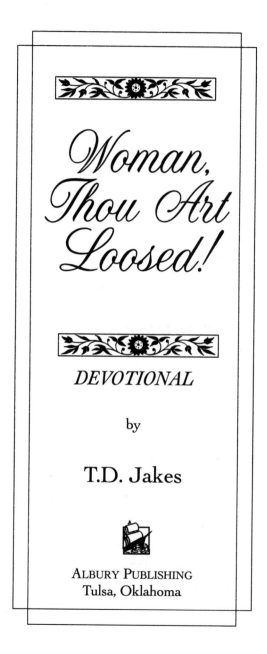

Woman, Thou Art Loosed!

DEVOTIONAL

by

T.D. Jakes

ALBURY PUBLISHING
Tulsa, Oklahoma

Scripture quotations are taken from the *King James Version* of the Bible.

Woman, Thou Art Loosed! Devotional
ISBN 1-57778-020-5
Copyright © 1997 by T.D. Jakes
P.O. Box 210887
Dallas, Texas 75211

Published by Albury Publishing
P.O. Box 470406
Tulsa, Oklahoma 74147-0406

TO

all the women from across the world who have received healing and restoration through the "Woman Thou Art Loosed" message. Your healing has made my life more meaningful. It is my prayer that this devotional assist you in keeping the chains of the past from refastening themselves in your life. When all is said and done you are a significant part of the pulse beat of God's divine purpose in the earth. Maintain your focus and whatever you do...keep moving!

~ Contents ~

8

Part VI

Loosed to Live in the Now

It's Time for You to Be Loosed!

Someone once said to me, "I heard about your *Woman, Thou Art Loosed!* presentation. The Bible tells us that in Christ there is no male or female. You ought to just preach, *Thou Art Loosed.*" I said to this person, "I think I'm going to continue to say what Jesus said." And what Jesus said is, "Woman, thou art loosed."

One of the issues that we must come to grips with is that those of us who are born again do not have a problem in our spirit. If we have been truly born again, our essence — what I call our "is-ness" — has been changed. We have been given an incorruptible nature in our spirit and we are forever changed.

The problem lies in our soul — that part of us that gives rise to our minds, emotions, memories, affections, and desires. If we were only spirit, we would have no need to be loosed of anything once we were born again. But we are not just spirit. We still live in a fleshly body and we have a worldly soul that needs to be transformed. That is a process that continues after our salvation experience.

11

Some of those things that tie up a woman in her soul are directly related to her feminine heart. They are part of her feminine nature, not her spirit.

God wants to loose something in the souls of women today. There's something He desires to set free. I believe that today is the day God wants to loose you in your heart,

> your attitude,
> your emotions,
> your spirit,
> your finances,
> your marriage,
> your work,
> your ministry,
> your praise.

He wants you to experience a freedom in Him — a freedom from temptation,

sin,

guilt,

things that are past,

relationships that are over

in order that you might LIVE.

God has a healing for your thoughts,

your emotions,

your attitudes.

He desires to heal you completely.

And then once you are loosed and made whole, His desire is that you never,

ever,

ever,

ever

go back into
bondage again.
Jesus wants to make you whole.
Are you willing to let Him do His work in you?

Part I

Loosed From Poor Self-Image

ᵔ *An Unwanted Woman* ᵔ

Leah was the elder daughter of Laban and the older sister of Rachel. She was the ugly duckling in the family, the "old maid." When Jacob went to work for Laban, he fell in love with Rachel and was willing to work seven long years to have her as his wife. Laban, however, tricked Jacob into marrying Leah first and then he required seven *more* years of labor from Jacob for Rachel. Leah was the unwanted bride, a woman scorned in favor of her beautiful, younger sister.

God, however, had a plan and purpose for Leah. He had created her for a divine role in His eternal plan and when He saw that Leah was despised by Jacob, He opened her womb and allowed her to bear children. In all, she bore six sons and one daughter — her sons became the founders of six of the twelve tribes of Israel.

From the Scriptures:

And Laban had two daughters: the name of the elder was Leah, and the name of the younger was Rachel.

Leah was tender eyed; but Rachel was beautiful and well favoured.

And Jacob loved Rachel; and said, I will serve thee seven years for Rachel thy younger daughter.

And Laban said, It is better that I give her to thee, than that I should give her to another man: abide with me.

And Jacob served seven years for Rachel; and they seemed unto him but a few days, for the love he had to her.

And Jacob said unto Laban, Give me my wife, for my days are fulfilled, that I may go in unto her.

And Laban gathered together all the men of the place, and made a feast.

And it came to pass in the evening, that he took Leah his daughter, and brought her to him; and he went in unto her.

And Laban gave unto his daughter Leah Zilpah his maid for an handmaid.

And it came to pass, that in the morning, behold, it was Leah: and he said to Laban, What is this thou hast done unto me? did not I serve with thee for Rachel? wherefore then hast thou beguiled me?

And Laban said, It must not be so done in our country, to give the younger before the first born.

Fulfil her week, and we will give thee this also for the service which thou shalt serve with me yet seven other years.

And Jacob did so, and fulfilled her week: and he gave him Rachel his daughter to wife also.

And Laban gave to Rachel his daughter Bilhah his handmaid to be her maid.

And he went in also unto Rachel, and he loved also Rachel more than Leah, and served with him yet seven other years.

And when the LORD saw that Leah was hated, he opened her womb: but Rachel was barren.

And Leah conceived, and bare a son, and she called his name Reuben.

— Genesis 29:16–32

✍ One ✍

You Are a Designer's Original

I will praise thee; for

I am fearfully and

wonderfully made:

marvellous are thy

works; and that

my soul knoweth

right well.

— Psalm 139:14

One of the things that makes the high-fashion designs of the New York and Paris designers so expensive is that they are one-of-a-kind creations. A woman who buys a *haute couture* design from the House of Chanel or Yves St. Laurant knows that she isn't going to see her dress on any other woman. She knows that she is going to own a garment that is superbly crafted, in many cases hand-stitched and custom-tailored to fit her like a soft leather glove fits a hand. She knows that every aspect of the design of her garment has been carefully conceived and crafted. She is willing to pay a high price for owning an original design.

19

And so it *should* be when we look at our own lives. God has put us together in a way that cannot be replicated and should not be replicated. He chose every aspect of our personalities, crafted every gift and talent He bestowed on us, and gave special thought to every one of our features and traits. We were handcrafted by Him in our mother's womb. He custom-made us to fit a specific role in His sovereign plan for the ages.

Leah was created and crafted and chosen for a specific purpose in God's plan, even though for much of her life she didn't know that.

She was a "designer's original."

And so are you.

God made you to be one of a kind.

Your fingerprint is different than that of anybody else — not only anybody else alive today but anybody else who has ever lived.

The same goes for your hand print,

footprint,

voice print,

20

and your entire genetic code. Nobody else has ever had the combination of physical traits that you have. Nobody else has precisely your set of genes.

And even if you did have the exact genetic makeup as another person, you would still be unique. Nobody else has been placed by God in *exactly*

your family,

in your neighborhood,

to have your friends and acquaintances,

in your city and state,

or to be a part of your church. Nobody else like you has been put on the earth at exactly this moment in history. Nobody else has had the exact set of experiences that you have had in your life. Nobody else has the same set of talents and personality quirks and strengths and weaknesses and abilities and disabilities and skills and training and connections that you have.

God designed you to live in a physical body that is especially adapted to this earth. He designed you with a specific number of hairs on your head and heartbeats in your heart. He knows the length of your days and the outer limits of your potential. He designed you with facets and dimensions that you may not even know!

God didn't create you to be static and unchanging. He made you with the ability to grow

> and to develop
> and to change
> and to adapt.

Only God does not change. People change. We age whether we want to or not. We perspire whether we want to or not.

As part of your ability to change and grow, God gave you the power of free will — the power to choose and to make decisions and to exert your own creativity. He gave you the ability to *change* how you think about God and about how you think about yourself. In other words, God gave you the ability to turn from sin and turn to Him. He gave you the ability to repent of the sins of your past and to walk in the paths of holiness.

Nobody else is put together exactly as you have been put together by God. Nobody has *ever* been just like you. And nobody will ever be just like you.

God doesn't repeat Himself.

21

Therefore . . .

Since there are no other women who could possibly be you, you may as well go ahead and be you, and think it's good to be you!

Have you developed an appreciation for your own individuality? Do you like the you that God designed you to be?

Do you wait for someone else to give you a compliment? Or, can you look at yourself in the mirror and say, "Good God of mercy, that's a fine-looking person in that mirror. If I don't have it going on this morning then I don't know how to get it going!"

Have you ever celebrated yourself? Have you ever praised God for the way He made you? If not, today is a good day to start!

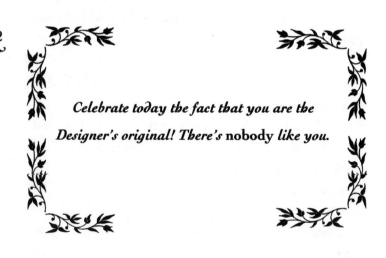

Celebrate today the fact that you are the Designer's original! There's nobody like you.

✍ Two ✍

There's No Comparison!

Leah was tender eyed; but Rachel was beautiful and well favoured.

— Genesis 29:17

Leah . . . but Rachel.

Leah and Rachel were compared. Not by God. Not according to who they were on the inside. Leah and Rachel were compared by people according to who they were on the outside.

God never asks us to compare ourselves with any other person. In fact, it is a slap in God's face to look at another person and say, "I wish I was more like her."

Why? Because God tenderly and uniquely designed you to be just the way He wanted you to be. He made you for Himself. He made you in a way that can never be duplicated.

When you begin to compare yourself to another person you are saying to God, "God, You made a mistake. You failed in making me. You could have done a better job in creating me." None of us has the privilege or right to criticize God in that way. He is the Creator who looks at each of His created beings and says to Himself, "It is good."

I am always amazed that women who are so concerned about making certain that they never wear the same dress that another woman is wearing to a special

23

function or to a church service, and who will go through all kinds of hairstyle and makeup changes to make sure that they don't appear to be copying someone else's "look," fail to apply that same principle to the way they see their own bodies, personalities, abilities, and inner attractiveness. They wouldn't dream of copying the way another woman dresses, but they desire to copy the way she is and to duplicate the way she acts, the way she talks, the way she performs, and the things that she has.

The fact is, everybody is attractive in one way or another.

The tragedy related to developing our own sense of attractiveness is twofold: we compare ourselves to others, and we allow others to define for us what is attractive.

It is dangerous to give that much power to another person — so that their opinion affects your own self-esteem and their definition becomes so contagious that if they do not affirm you, you don't affirm yourself.

We each must get to the place where we hold a high opinion of ourselves solely on the basis of the fact that God made us

exactly,

precisely,

intricately,

wondrously,

and uniquely the way we are. Each of us is a one-of-a-kind creation for which there is no comparison!

God made you for His own purposes in order that you might reflect a unique aspect of His own glory.

24

Are you so busy scrutinizing your faults and failures that you fail to recognize your uniqueness?

Are you so busy studying and analyzing somebody else that you fail to appreciate what God has given you?

Are you so busy trying to change yourself that you have neglected to praise God for who He made you to be in the first place?

When you cease to compare yourself to others and refuse to be intimidated by what other people think and say, you are then in the position to

birth that business that God wants you to birth,

birth that ministry that God wants you to birth,

birth that effort to change your

community that God wants you to birth.

How dare you compare yourself to somebody else! God wanted you to be you. Nobody else. YOU!

25

Thank God today for making you exactly the way you are and for transforming you day by day into exactly the woman He wants YOU to be. You are without comparison in His eyes!

~ *Three* ~

God Had a Good Idea

Blessed be the God and Father of our Lord Jesus Christ, who hath blessed us with all spiritual blessings in heavenly places in Christ: According as he hath chosen us in him before the foundation of the world, that we should be holy and without blame before him in love.

— Ephesians 1:3–4

How does a designer work?

I've never watched a fashion designer create a garment but I suspect the process is exactly like that of any other person who creates something that hasn't existed before.

The first step in the process is an idea. The designer no doubt "sees" with his mind's eye what his design will look like. He may then sketch out that design or start to work with fabrics to fold and drape them to bring his design to life.

You were created in the mind of God before you were put into a womb. You were God's *idea.*

Leah was God's idea before she was ever Laban's daughter, or Rachel's sister, or Jacob's wife. Her very definition and identity came from God. And so does your identity. You are God's idea, God's choice, God's creation.

And God is the One who *made* you for a specific time and place on this earth.

You aren't an accident,

    a mistake,

    an error,

    an incident,

    or a mishap.

You were fashioned and made by Elohim — the Lord God Almighty, Creator of heaven and earth. You were meticulously and distinctly made by the Master. There are many people today who grew up hearing that they weren't wanted by their parents. They were told that they were the result of a "careless moment." If you have been told that, you need to take this position: I disagree.

Your parents may have been careless, but God was very careful. You weren't born because of something your parents did or didn't do. You were born because of something that God did in your mother's womb. He is the One who caused you to be born. He is the One who allowed that one sperm cell to enter that one egg cell for life to begin. He is the One who mixed together the genes of your mother and the genes of your father to give you an identity that is distinctly different from that of either your mother or father! He is the One who breathed life into you and caused you to come into being.

27

Your mother and your father didn't create you. God created you. Your mother and father set up a situation in which God had the prerogative to create or not to create. They set up a circumstance in which God had the option to make you then or to wait and make you at another moment in time. But it is God who *made* you. You are *His* creation. And God doesn't make mistakes. He doesn't err. He doesn't have mishaps or incidents or accidents. God creates only what He wants to create.

You can't force the hand of God. You can't demand that God create when He doesn't want to create. He is who He is . . . and He made you to be who He wanted on the earth as His person in a particular time and place to do a particular job.

God could have put you into any body

of any age and

of any race

at any time

in any place that He chose. His idea for you, however, was that you be put precisely into *your* mother's body, and that you emerge at a designated hour and day and year in a specific location. He held back His idea of you "for such a time as this." He brought you into this world through a specific set of situations and circumstances, and then He raised you up through another set of specific situations and circumstances, for one great purpose — to complete *His* purpose and reflect *His* glory.

It doesn't matter if you were conceived during an act of date rape and born to a welfare mother who had thirteen other children by ten different men. God is the One who ordained and authorized your birth. He created you for His purposes and His glory.

He didn't allow you to be aborted or to be miscarried. He didn't allow you to be stillborn or to die of crib death. He didn't allow any number of childhood accidents or diseases to take you out. He intended from the very first moment that He had the *idea* for you that you should live and participate in His plan and accomplish His purposes.

He never took His hand off your life. It doesn't matter if you were abused as a child. God brought you through that experience alive and He is the One who kept you from losing your sanity. He is the One who brought you to an understanding of Jesus Christ as your Savior and raised you up so that you could *still* fulfill His purposes and reflect His glory in *spite* of every effort the devil made against you to destroy you, diminish you, defame you, or discourage you.

The fact is . . . if you hadn't gone through every thing that you have gone through, you wouldn't *be* the person you are today. And God knows that! He has been in the process of creating you,

> fashioning you,
> molding you,
> designing you,
> refining you,
> and perfecting you

since the moment before the foundations of the earth when He first thought of you!

He gave you your own personality,

> your own abilities,
> your own set of spiritual gifts,
> and your own identity in Christ so

that you and you alone might

> praise the way you praise,
> give what you give,

29

minister like you minister,
and love like you love.
Oh yes! When God thought of you, He had a *good* idea.

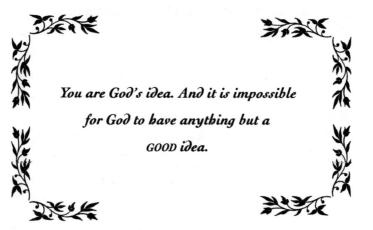

You are God's idea. And it is impossible for God to have anything but a GOOD idea.

Four

Your Inner and Outer Beauty

Whose adorning let it not be that outward adorning of plaiting the hair, and of wearing of gold, or of putting on of apparel; but let it be the hidden man of the heart, in that which is not corruptible, even the ornament of a meek and quiet spirit, which is in the sight of God of great price.

— 1 Peter 3:3–4

When a designer sends a model down the runway of a fashion show, he or she is concerned with the total look of the model. The model isn't just wearing the designer's garment. The designer, in nearly all cases, has spent a great deal of time and effort to make sure the model is wearing the right accessories — the right jewelry or shoes or hat. Most designers pay very close attention to the hairstyles and makeup of their models. They also tell them how to walk and turn and carry themselves. And they create the overall environment in which the models are to model their designs.

And so it with our great God. He created you as a composite. He put certain talents and features together with specific

31

personality traits, and then He added various emotional responses and spiritual gifts. He was concerned with the overall, total you. He designed you to be a vibrant,

thinking,

feeling,

fully functioning person

who has a unique attractiveness. He adorned you with far more than physical appearance.

In the early days of the Pentecostal Movement, we made a serious mistake, in my opinion, in asking women to avoid all self-adornment. Women were admonished not to wear jewelry or short sleeves in their dresses or to style their hair in any way other than in a bun or covered with a prayer cap. The leaders of the movement were so concerned with the development of the inner qualities of a woman that they failed to recognize that the way a woman expresses herself in the physical and natural realm is a part of her creativity and uniqueness.

When the next generation of Pentecostals came along, they seemed to rebel against this lack of self-adornment and they went to the other extreme. Church services almost became a fashion show — each woman eyeing and appraising the hat and dress and jewelry and shoes of the woman sitting next to her in the pew. We seemed to take outer appearance and adornment as a sign that God was blessing us. We justified our clothes and furs and jewels as being a part of our witness of God's prosperity.

What we need is balance.

God made us with flesh — an outer appearance. God has blessed us with creativity and an appreciation for beauty. We can and should recognize our appearance as an area in which we express ourselves to the glory of God.

God also made us with inner qualities — gifts and talents and traits and personalities — that are also intended to be developed and displayed *to the glory of God*.

The outer doesn't replace the need for the inner. The inner doesn't negate the need for the outer. We must have balance. And, we must always recognize that the inner qualities are those which are eternal and therefore, the more important. It is the inner qualities that should give rise to the outer ones. In other words, it is who we are on the *inside* that should define for each of us what we choose to do with our *outside*.

That didn't happen in Leah's case. She was judged only by what she looked like on the outside. Nobody saw the total Leah, except God.

Some women make that same mistake today. They define themselves by what they wear and how they look. If they have a bad hair day, they are in a rotten mood all day. If they get a run in their hose, they lose their self-confidence. They allow the outer appearance to determine their inner demeanor.

God's plan for us is just the opposite — it is the inner demeanor that should dictate and define how we adorn ourselves. The woman who is self-confident in the Lord on the inside might choose to wear a $1.50 dress that she finds at the local thrift shop or a $150 dress that she buys at an upscale department store. She is self-confident either way. Her look doesn't determine her character. No . . . her character is intact in spite of her look.

Every one of us must recognize that the greater part of our attractiveness cannot be

bought,

taken off a rack or shelf,

applied like a lipstick,

or put on like a hat or shoes. The greater part of our attractiveness lies within and it wells up from the inside and finds a creative and appropriate expression on the outside.

That's what Peter meant when he wrote that "the ornament of a meek and quiet spirit" is what has a "great price" in the sight of God. (See 1 Peter 3:4.)

God sees what no one else can see. And it's that part of you that He values the most.

34

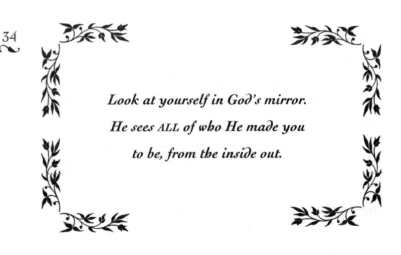

Look at yourself in God's mirror.
He sees ALL of who He made you
to be, from the inside out.

❧ Five ❧

The Wellspring of Your Attractiveness

> *Be strengthened with might by his Spirit in the inner man.*
>
> — Ephesians 3:16

The greater part of your attractiveness — the part that draws or *attracts* other people to you — is on the inside, not on your flesh.

Have you ever seen a woman walking on the arm of a man and you asked yourself, "How on earth did *she get him?*" Did you think, "If *she* got somebody, surely Lord, You can do that for me!"

One day a woman flew across the nation to meet with me. She wanted to tell me her story — how her husband had left her for another woman and was tied up in an affair. The woman who came to see me was young, vibrant, beautiful — she met all the standards of what we would call a clean-living, godly woman. She sat weeping in my office and then in her frustration as she told me what had happened, she opened up her pocketbook and pulled out a photograph and said to me, "Just look at her!"

I didn't want to look . . . I didn't *need* to look in order to understand what was happening. She insisted. "Just *look* at her! He left me for *that*!"

35

I said, "The tragedy, ma'am, is that what you have been trained by our society to think is important, really isn't all that important. Appearance doesn't mean all that you think it does. Outer appearance isn't always the issue."

If you don't believe that, I encourage you to go to the nearest mall and sit for a while and watch the people go by. You'll see some of the strangest couples holding hands!

Our society spends billions of dollars a year to convince you to buy hundreds, even thousands of dollars a year worth of clothes and makeup in order to fix up something that doesn't really matter all that much. We spend countless hours at beauty salons and spas and malls in order to buy, acquire, or create the very things that we *think* will draw other people to us, but which actually have very little drawing power. What you create or design on the outside of yourself may turn a head or two, but it has very little power to turn a mind or a heart.

We are bombarded on a daily basis with messages that tell us that if we only

go to the right weight-loss center

and get down to the right size

and dye our hair the right shade

and go to the right spa

and use the right toothpaste

and put on the right makeup

and wear the right outfit

    at the right time

and be seen in the right places

    with the right people

then we most certainly will be able to get for ourselves the

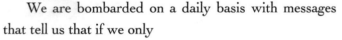

right man

and have the right children
and live in the right neighborhood
and enjoy the right kind of life!

When we do this and nothing "right" happens for us, we are puzzled. We sit back and ask, "What went wrong?"

What went wrong was this — we became merchandise for those who were selling us merchandise!

The average woman — yes, even the average Christian woman — will spend literally thousands of dollars this year on

hats
and nails
and tints
and weaves
and earrings
and dresses

and sadly, spend virtually nothing to build up and support those inner qualities and character traits that truly are what attract others to us

. . . and to Jesus Christ our Savior.

If you are only concerned with your outer appearance, you are going to be a very shallow, superficial person. People are going to find that once they have quit playing with you, the box in which you came was beautifully wrapped . . . but it was empty.

Now, I believe in women looking good. If you were to ask my wife about this, she would tell you that I spare no expense in helping her look good. I want her to look as

37

good as she can look. Not only do I appreciate looking at her, but I like the way people look at *us* when we are out together. When she's looking good, she makes me look better than I otherwise look! Most men know this, by the way. They know they look better to other people when they are seen in public with a woman who has a great-looking outer appearance.

What most women don't know about most men, however, is that outer looks don't matter nearly as much as inner qualities once that man is home alone with his wife.

I did not marry my wife for her good looks. I married her for her *self.* Her *self* included far more than her good looks.

Shortly after my wife and I married, my wife was in an automobile accident. Her ankle was badly crushed. The doctors told us that she might never walk again. Now, I love the way my wife walks, but when the doctors told me that my wife might never walk again, I wasn't devastated. I was just glad my wife was still alive. I was glad she still had all her inner qualities that drew me to marry her in the first place.

For the better part of that next year, I carried my wife just about every place she went. She was in such pain she could hardly move. When she needed to wash her hair, I carried a basin of warm water to her as she lay on the sofa and I helped her hang her head over the side of the sofa so she could shampoo her hair.

The doctors finally said she might walk again but not without a metal brace up to her knee. I thanked the doctors for their opinion but then I looked the devil right in the eye and said, "You are a liar." I refused to accept that diagnosis from the doctors as the final verdict.

When my wife started to take her first few tentative steps, I'd encourage her, "Just take one step. Now just take one more." Over the process of months, I helped her learn how to walk again.

She is now wearing high heels . . . and she has her walk back! She is dancing in the aisles and praising God.

As much as I was convinced in my spirit that my wife *would* walk again, I also faced the possibility in my mind that she might not. God calls us to have faith, not to be unrealistic or to live in a state of denial. And in facing the possibility that my wife might not walk, I made up my mind while my wife was lying in her bed that if she *never* walked again, I would push her around in a wheelchair and love her just the same as if she was walking by my side. Her ability to walk didn't have anything to do with my ability to love.

39

Go back to the SOURCE of what it is that makes you "attract" other people — the Source of your attractiveness is the Holy Spirit of God. He is the One who woos and wins the heart. When you are His woman, He will draw to you

the right people

for the right purposes

at just the right time!

Trust God today to be the wellspring of your attractiveness.

The most attractive part of you
is deep within you,
just waiting to be expressed.

40

Six

Agreeing With God's Opinion of You

And God saw every

thing that he had

made, and, behold, it

was very good.

— Genesis 1:31

God looked. He saw you. He saw everything He had created around you.

He saw the reason for your being.

He saw a specific need on this earth that you were to meet.

He saw the full set of traits and abilities that you would need to have in order to complete your purpose for living.

He knew what kind of environment you would need in order to develop your traits and abilities.

God looked, and then He created.

He created you.

You!

And God looked at you and said, "This is *good*."

Do you have that same opinion of yourself? Do you agree with God's opinion of the way He made you?

It's important that you come to appreciate the way God created you because other people are going to treat

41

you the way you treat yourself. They will respect you only to the degree that you respect yourself.

Have you ever purchased a gift for somebody who is really particular? It's a job. You can't just run to the local bargain basement and snatch the first thing you see. You know that the person doesn't settle for just anything so you spend the time to get something for her that you believe she'd choose for herself. If you truly care about a person, you tend to buy for that person the things that you think she would buy for herself. The higher the standards she has for herself, the higher the standards you place on the gift you choose.

If you are attracting people who don't treat you well, the first suspect in the case is *you*. What kind of message are you sending that allows them to treat you poorly?

There must be something deep inside of you that sends out a signal, "I *am* somebody because God made me to be somebody. I may not be twenty-one and wear a size seven. I may be seventy-one and wear a size twenty-seven. But I *am* somebody."

When you send out a signal like that, then that is the signal other people pick up.

There's something that you exude out of your spirit that gives you presence with others. There's a quality of inner strength that gives you an attraction. It causes other people to recognize you,

to pay attention to you,

to ask when you walk into the room, "Who is that?" They won't be asking because of the garment you are wearing, but rather, because of the strength of character that you project.

That attitude is not arrogance or pride. It is healthy self-esteem and the strength of God's Spirit inside you.

I once watched a woman approach a clerk in an office and ask in a weak, self-deprecating voice, "I don't want to bother you, but if you could please . . ." This woman was sending the message, "I know you won't like me and don't want to deal with me and don't think highly of me." She had an attitude of apology for who God made her to be.

And what happened? The clerk in that office treated her just the way she projected that she *expected* to be treated. She got walked on, sent off to sit in a corner for half an hour, and talked down to in a rude, put-down manner.

The way you appreciate yourself impacts everything you do. It affects the way that you

    sit in a classroom

        or apply for a job

            or talk to people at a social
            function

                or go about the ministry

that God has called you to undertake. It even affects the way that you pray and the way that you study God's Word. If you think that you are a nobody with no future and no value, you are going to pray with less power and think that the promises of God are for everybody else but you.

God's desire is that you appreciate who He made you to be and to develop what He gave you — not that you try

43

to exchange what He gave you for what He gave someone else.

Don't let anybody ever convince you that you should change yourself to be like someone else. I once heard about a woman who married a man and then after she got married, she decided that her husband would love her even more if she changed just about everything about her that could be changed. What happened? One day he woke up and said, "Who are you?" She had changed herself so much that he no longer recognized her as the person he had married.

From her perspective, she looked better, dressed better, and was more polished. From his perspective, she had become a stranger.

She had worried about some woman coming along and catching her husband's eye. What she hadn't accepted was that he only had eyes for her in the first place. She hadn't been able to fully receive his love and approval because she hadn't approved of herself.

You must also be wary if somebody begins to date you or marries you and then starts to demand that you change things about yourself to conform to what *they* think you ought to look like,

talk like,

act like,

or dress like. That person doesn't want what God created. He wants to do the creating. You're better off sticking with what God created you to be than to substitute that for what some person tries to create. Another person can never create you to be as good as what God has made.

Now, there are lots of people that I admire. I may admire some of their attributes or think they look wonderful or appreciate the way they do certain things. But I have never met anyone who had anything about them that I found so wonderful or so intimidating that I was willing to give up being ME in order to try to be THEM. No way!

Furthermore, you must develop deep within yourself the capacity and the tenacity to disagree with those who feel differently about you than you feel about you.

You must be able to say to another person . . .

You don't approve of me?

You don't like the way I look?

You don't like the way I talk?

You don't think I'm a quality person?

You don't think I have value?

You don't think I am worthy?

You don't think I have a purpose and reason for being that's just as important as that of the next person?

I disagree!

You don't have to get mad about it,

argue the point,

fight over the facts,

or spend the rest of your life trying to prove that you're right and they're wrong. You simply disagree. You take the position, That's *your* position. That's not *my* position. And just before you walk away, you simply and calmly say, "You have your opinion, but I

45

also have mine. I disagree with your opinion. I like me. I value me. And I *know* God does, too."

It's time for you to look yourself and others in the eye and say with your attitude, if not your words:

Excuse me, but I have a right to be myself.

Excuse me, but I have the right to express myself.

Excuse me, but I have the right to have my opinions.

Excuse me, but I have the right to use my faith.

Excuse me, but I choose to agree with what God has said about me!

46

Value yourself today the way God values you — beyond measure!

Seven

The Call for You

I know thee by name, and thou hast also found grace in my sight.

— Exodus 33:12

A popular love song from a number of years ago was titled "Only You." Some of us need to go back and sing that song — to ourselves.

There's a role that God has for "only you." Nobody else will do.

In the theater world, actors and actresses often go for auditions and then the director or producer of the play or movie will have callbacks. Certain ones of those who have auditioned will be asked to come back and have a second, and sometimes a third or fourth audition before they are given the part or they are told that someone else has won the role.

A person in the entertainment world knows that he or she has arrived as a star when a director or producer calls them and offers them the part *without* an audition. They are being chosen for who they are to fill a role that the director believes is absolutely perfect for them and nobody else.

Leah had a role that only Leah could fill. Nobody else. When God asked, "Who should be the mother of Reuben and Simeon and Levi and Judah and Issachar

47

and Zebulun and Dinah?" He came up with only one name: Leah.

God doesn't deal in auditions and call backs for His children. He has something for you to do that *only* you can do. There's nobody else who can play the part or fill the role or meet the need or match the qualifications required. Only *you*.

If a person just wants a "woman," then you have a lot of competition. But when the call goes out for you, you have *no* competition. Only you can truly be you.

When people call and invite me to come and do seminars, I make sure that the person they really want is T. D. Jakes.

Do they just want a preacher?

Do they just want somebody to put on the program?

Do they just want somebody who has been on television or written a book?

I want to make sure they really want ME.

Because, you see, I know from the depths of my spirit that nobody can be ME as good as I can be me!

I never worry about anybody coming along and being a better T. D. than me. I am absolutely awesome at being T. D. Jakes. I have a doctorate degree in being me. There are no contenders in being me.

When you choose me, you get me. I am not a copy of anybody. I am a designer's original.

Now wouldn't I be foolish if I tried to be Pastor White? I would never be as good a Pastor White as Pastor White can be Pastor White. I would only be a cheap copy. And I have absolutely no desire to be a cheap copy

when I can be a
    first-class,
        truly wonderful,
            incredibly good,
                perfectly equipped,
                    one-of-a-kind
                        original!

A person could study me for hours and still not do what I do. They could make me the sole object of their scrutiny for days and still never be able to be a better T. D. Jakes than I am T. D. Jakes. They simply cannot do what I do in being the me that God made me to be.

If somebody doesn't love you enough to love you in spite of how you look on the outside or what you are capable of doing in the flesh, then they don't really love you. They only love your flesh.

If a man only loves your figure
                or the way you do your hair
                or the way you sing
                or the way you dance
                or the way you laugh
then he does not really love you. He only loves the IMAGE of you. He is not in love with the real you, because the real you is a composite of what is on the inside and what is on the outside, and what is on the inside is the more important part.

Suppose you lose your voice?

Suppose you lose a limb and can't dance?

Suppose you lose your figure?

49

You want someone to love you first and foremost for what is in your spirit and in your soul, not what is draped on your body.

You want someone to love you for the twinkle in your eye, not for your expensive eye makeup.

You want someone to love you for the dimple on your cheek and the funny way your voice rises at the end of your laugh and your tender touch that is unlike that of any other woman.

You want someone who will recognize your voice even if he is blindfolded. You want someone who will know your touch even if he is blindfolded and put into a sound chamber. You want someone who will love you for the things that make you *you* — not for the things that make you look like the model in the fashion magazine or act like the person on a TV show.

What we each must do is wait for the call that is specifically for us.

We aren't to respond to a blanket call

or a generic call

or a gender call

or a wolf-whistle call,

but to a call that says, "I don't want anybody but *you* and the reason is that only *you* will do."

That is the call that is the one we should wait to hear from a person who wants to be our spouse. That's the call that is the one we should wait to hear from a person we make our friend.

That's the call that God puts on our lives. He calls us very individually — by name, not number — to do a very specific job and to fill a very specific role in His Kingdom. Nobody else will do. He has designed us to meet all the qualifications required. He hasn't created any other person that will fit the bill like we fit the bill.

You don't need to be jealous of or intimidated by anyone else because when God calls for you, there is nobody else who can answer that call. You have no contenders in His sight. You are the *star* He has in mind for the role He has written just for you.

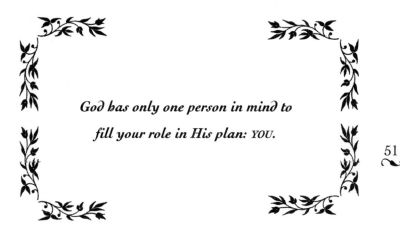

God has only one person in mind to fill your role in His plan: YOU.

51

Eight

God Still Has a Plan

When the LORD saw that Leah was hated, he opened her womb . . . and Leah conceived.

— Genesis 29:31–32

We each learn our own definition of beauty and attractiveness.

Attractiveness varies from culture to culture, from era to era, and from person to person. What is considered attractive to you may not be what I consider to be beautiful.

According to the definition of the times, Rachel was considered to be very beautiful — a bombshell, a fox. She was a rose petal, stardust, the tremor in the earthquake. The Bible says she was "well-favored." Jacob, it seems, looked at her and almost stopped breathing. Any time a man says that he is willing to work for seven years at doglike labor, that man is either in love or crazy.

Leah, whose name means gazelle, was older and lankier than her sister, and knobby and "tender eyed." My grandmother would have said cockeyed. She very likely had an orbital or lazy eye. She may have been cross-eyed.

Don't start putting down Leah, however. She was God's woman, especially chosen for a specific job.

Rachel's treasure was on her.

But Leah's treasure was in her.

People who never look in you are too shallow to appreciate what they will find there.

On the outside, it didn't look as if God had much of a plan for Leah.

Leah had been victimized. A girl's first definition of masculinity is formed when she looks at her father. Leah's father, Laban, didn't think much of her. He was almost like a pimp. He made a deal with a man for her and sold her for a favor. She was a "booby" prize, her father's joke on Jacob.

It's funny to read the story about how Laban tricked Jacob, giving Leah to him as a bride and Jacob not realizing it until the next morning. Laban then insisted that Jacob work an additional seven years — a total of fourteen years — for the privilege of having Rachel for his bride. The story is funny . . . until you look at it from Leah's point of view.

Can you imagine how Leah must have felt as she got ready for her wedding, knowing that she was about to be married off as a joke, a booby prize? Can you imagine how she felt, having waited all her life to be loved by a man, knowing that her groom didn't want her but wanted her younger sister instead? Leah no doubt had her hopes and dreams as a young woman, but in marrying Jacob, she knew that those hopes and dreams would never be realized.

53

Leah spent the entire night with Jacob, who never realized who she was until the following morning. She was intimate with a man who didn't really know who she was. He
never looked her in the eye, much less into her soul. He
wanted only what he wanted — he had no regard or respect
for the total God-designed composite whole of Leah.

Have you ever been in an intimate relationship with
someone who didn't really know who you were — someone who only wanted your body?

Have you worked on a job with someone who didn't
really know who you were — and didn't make any effort
to find out? Have you ever been involved in ministry with
someone who didn't know who you were, not really, and
who didn't care enough to take the time to find out who
you were? It's a terrible situation to be in.

And then to make matters even worse, when Jacob
found that he had been with Leah, he still wanted someone else.

54

Year after year, Leah was married to a man who was
looking at someone else, who wanted someone else. Leah
was still the invisible woman as far as Jacob was concerned. She may have done the chores around the tent and
he may have used her for sex, but his desire was for Rachel.

No, Jacob didn't see Leah. But God did.

And God sees you.

You are not invisible to Him.

You are not unknown to Him.

You are not a mystery to Him.

He *still* has a plan and a purpose for your life. He still has something that He has put in you that He desires to bring to fruition.

God sees you and He intends for others not only to see you but receive from you the hidden treasure He put inside you.

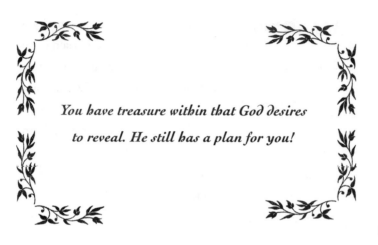

You have treasure within that God desires to reveal. He still has a plan for you!

～ Nine ～

Overcoming a Generational Curse

Weeping may

endure for a night,

but joy cometh in

the morning.

— Psalm 30:5

We all know that certain physical characteristics are passed from generation to generation. A physician may ask you to give him not only your personal health history, but also that of your parents and grandparents. Did they have high blood pressure? Did they have kidney disease? And so forth. Certain physical ailments and diseases seem linked to our ancestors.

The same is true for some emotional characteristics. Some families are riddled with divorce. It seems everybody on the family tree got a divorce. Some families seem to be very powerful or financially successful generation after generation. Other families seem to have lived on welfare for generations. Some families can point to ten or more women in their family who have had babies out of wedlock.

From generation to generation, we see rage and abuse. Even those who were abused and know how painful abuse can be, have a tendency to abuse their own children whom they claim to love.

We might call these generational curses. We act out our father's sins.

Jacob's family was riddled with problems. His grandmother Sarah had been a schemer — advising Abraham to have a baby by Hagar, and then sending Hagar away. His grandfather Abraham had also used some tricks, especially in trying to convince important and powerful men that Sarah was really his sister and not his wife. His mother Rebekah had been a schemer — advising her favorite son Jacob to steal both the birthright and the blessing from Jacob's twin brother Esau.

Jacob's very name meant supplanter, trickster, con man. The ability to be "slick" was something his mother saw in him from his birth, probably because she knew what it meant to be slick herself. After Jacob had tricked his father Isaac into giving him what rightfully belonged to Esau, Rebekah sent him away to the home of her brother Laban — another trickster.

Laban was slick in the family tradition. He conned Jacob into working seven years for Rachel, and then gave him Leah instead. It was a trick, a con. And out of the con, he tricked Jacob into working seven more years.

Manipulators have a need to be in control, regardless of the cost. Laban wanted labor from Jacob. He wanted to control his life, even if it meant giving up his daughters in the process. The moment that Laban realized that Jacob was madly in love with Rachel, Laban knew the

57

weakness in Jacob that he could manipulate. He controlled Jacob for fourteen years.

Leah grew up surrounded by tricksters and manipulated by them.

What is a woman to do in a situation like that?

She must choose not to give in to the generational curse.

You see, a person who manipulates others is a person who says, "I need to con my way into what I don't deserve and cannot earn." The way the curse is broken is to say, "God is capable of using who I am and what I have."

A little boy only had five loaves and two fishes. Jesus said, "Let me have them. I can make do with them."

A woman said I have only a little meal and a bit of oil. Elijah said, "Let me have them. That's just enough for God to make a miracle."

A woman said, "I only have one small cruse of oil." The prophet said, "Here's what God wants you to do with it."

God can take whatever it is that you have — even if it's only a little bit — and multiply it into a miracle. It can be more than enough for you to fulfill what it is that God wants you to do.

A woman once worked in an office. She was a terrible typist. She kept making mistakes and she was spending all of her time correcting them. She needed her job so she said, "I've got to do something about this." She said to herself, "I don't have all the typing skills in the world but I am a pretty good problem-solver and a pretty good artist." So she went home and began to experiment with some of her art supplies until she created the product we have come to call "white out." She became a millionaire — not because of what she *couldn't* do, but because she was willing to use what she *could* do.

You don't need a lot of talent. You only need a little bit.

Are you aware that there are models who are hired to do commercials and appear in advertisements who have only one good feature — it might be her hands or her legs or her feet or her eyes? She'll be hired for close-up shots of that one good feature, even though the rest of her may not be all that beautiful. She has found the little bit that God gave her. She's working it!

Many people are in financial trouble today because they have no confidence in the little bit that God has given them. They are waiting for manna to fall from heaven instead of working with what God has already given. I have news for them — that dispensation of manna-giving is over. God expects us to trust Him with what He has given us — and to use what He has given us — to get what it is that we need and want.

Every time I meet with a group of women, I sense an abundance of treasure that God wants to release. Each one of them has something that God is eager to bless and multiply. God wants each one to recognize what He has given them — even if it's only a little bit — and start working with what they have.

Quit crying over where you've been.

Quit crying over your mistakes and failures.

Quit crying over what you have lost.

Start looking toward where you are going.

Start looking toward what God has for you.

Start looking for what God is going to give you as a blessing.

Start looking for the way God is going to use what you do have.

Leah had just enough of what it was that God needed most. And so do you.

You don't need to con or scheme your way into your future. Give God what you have and let Him do the miracle of fulfillment in you and for you.

Releasing the Hidden Treasure Within You

We have this treasure

in earthen vessels,

that the excellency of

the power may

be of God.

— 2 Corinthians 4:7

Leah had gifts and abilities — hidden treasure — but Jacob could never see it.

The Bible says that when the Lord saw how Leah was hated, He opened her womb. (See Genesis 29:31.) When God saw how Leah was mistreated and despised, He opened up the hidden treasure that lay inside of Leah and brought it forth.

There's something in you that has been locked up that God wants to unlock today.

61

God knows what He has put in you. He knows what He desires to come out of you. And He knows how to get to what He has put in you and bring it out of you.

When you get beyond your low self-esteem and you stop comparing yourself to other people, and you begin to face and accept what God has given *you,* then you are in a position for God to bring to birth *all* that He has created you to be.

There are things in you that have been overlooked by you,

    ignored by others,

        perhaps even ridiculed by some,

            but God calls those traits in you treasure. And He wants to bring them forth!

He has given every woman treasure — something that He intends for her to use in order to fulfill her purpose on earth. And in the process of fulfilling her purpose and God's purpose, she will bring God glory.

You had better find out what it is that God has put in you as treasure . . . because the devil is going to fight you for what God has put in you. The devil knows that treasure is there and he wants it — he wants it bad — for his purposes.

So many women today are fighting the devil and they don't even know why. They haven't discovered the treasure that lies within them. The devil knows it's there. God knows it's there. So the fight is on and the woman doesn't even know what the fight is all about. Discover your treasure. The treasure in you is not only what the devil wants, but it is the way you will defeat the devil in your life.

The devil will do anything he can to sabotage your self-esteem so you won't use your treasure or assert your gift because he doesn't want you to give birth to what God has put within you.

Being loosed means that the treasure within you has been released. It means that the treasure that has been bound within you has been given an emancipation proclamation. It means that you are free to blossom and bring forth fruit! When the treasure within you is loosed, you are at liberty to give birth.

Now giving birth may require intense effort on your part. You may have to push like a woman in labor. You may have to fill your jaws with air and push with all your might against the devil.

The apostle Paul said, "Forgetting those things which are behind, and reaching forth unto those things which are before, I press toward the mark for the prize of the high calling of God in Christ Jesus" (Philippians 3:13–14). Pressing is pushing.

You may have to push against what happened to you when you were a child, what your teachers said about you on the first day of school, or what your first boyfriend did to you. You may have to push with all your might to release what it is that God has put within you. In fact, it may not happen if you don't push!

The doctors tell a woman to push because there's something inside her that is supposed to come out. The same is true for the treasure in you. There's something God-conceived and God-created in you that is *supposed* to come out.

63

You may have to battle through years of
suppression,

    oppression,

        and depression . . . but that which is within you is something God wants to bring to birth.

He put the treasure there. He'll help you bring the treasure out. But it is up to you to push.

Now what are you pushing against? You aren't pushing against other people. This isn't a battle in the natural.
It is a battle of the spirit. You are going to have to push
against the opposition of the devil. His opposition comes
in the form of bad memories, low self-esteem, and feelings
of being unworthy. The devil may have spent years pushing you aside, pulling you back, and putting you down.
Now the Lord says to you, "I've seen how the world has
hated you. I want to open you up. I want you to give birth
to that which I put in you."

It is time for you to say to yourself and the world as a
whole, "It's my time to conceive. It's time for the treasure
that God put inside me to come up. It's time for me to be
LOOSED to do what it is that God created me to do."

You may have to push against thoughts of suicide.
You may have to push against years of bitterness and
anger. You may have to push against your own feelings of
being intimidated.

You may have to push against your own tendency to
compare yourself to others. When you compare yourself
to other people, you restrict yourself to a spiritual barrenness. You allow yourself to become more concerned
about what people think of you than what the Spirit of
God wants to do in you and through you.

The treasure in you is filled with possibilities and
potentialities. Your treasure is a blessing that is just waiting to be birthed.

When a baby is birthed, it changes everything in the
family. The same is true for you. When you give birth to
the treasure that God has put in you, your entire life is

going to be changed. Your marriage will be affected. Your relationship with your children will be affected. Your place in your church and your neighborhood and your workplace is going to be affected. God's blessing is an overflowing blessing.

I'm talking about birthing the gifts
                                    and talents
                                                and powers
and the ministries of the Holy Spirit inside you. I don't know the specific thing that God wants to birth in you but you know what it is. Every woman knows when she is pregnant. In fact, a woman often has an inner knowing that she is pregnant, even before she has any feeling of the baby moving inside her womb. The same is true for the spiritual ministries that God has put inside you. There's a knowing that you have.

Don't fail today to give birth to what God put in you. NOW is the time for the baby — that treasure — to be born.

65

God has put in you something the whole world needs and is waiting for. PUSH!

~ *Eleven* ~

You Hold a Key to Deliverance

And the God of

peace shall bruise

Satan under your

feet shortly.

The grace of our

Lord Jesus Christ be

with you.

— Romans 16:20

66

Why is it so massively important that a woman give birth to what it is that God has put within her?

Because the woman holds the key to deliverance. It is the seed of the woman that was designated by God to rise up and bruise the heel of Satan. After Adam and Eve had sinned, God cursed the serpent that had tempted Eve with this curse:

"I will put enmity between thee and the woman, and between thy seed and her seed; it shall bruise thy head, and thou shalt bruise his heel" (Genesis 3:15). God trusted the woman with deliverance in her womb. There's been enmity between the devil and women ever since. Satan doesn't want you to bring to birth that which God has put inside you. Why? Because what you bring to birth has the potential to bruise his head!

You have

talents

    and gifts

        and resources within you that have the power to cause serious damage to what Satan is attempting to do in this world.

When the children of Israel were about to be taken to Babylon in bondage, the prophet Jeremiah said, "Send for the women of mourning." He said —

O daughter of my people, gird thee with sackcloth, and wallow thyself in ashes: make thee mourning, as for an only son, most bitter lamentation: for the spoiler shall suddenly come upon us. I have set thee for a tower and a fortress among my people (Jeremiah 6:26–27).

Jeremiah also said that the Lord of hosts had told him specifically to —

Call for the mourning women, that they may come . . . And let them make haste, and take up a wailing for us, that our eyes may run down with tears, and our eyelids gush out with waters. . . . O ye women . . . let your ear receive the word of his mouth, and teach your daughters wailing, and every one her neighbour lamentation. For death is come up into our windows, and is entered into our palaces, to cut off the children from without, and the young men from the streets (Jeremiah 9:17–18, 20–21).

Jeremiah said, "Find some women who are not so filled with hate and bitterness that they have become like mannequins, women who are not so downtrodden that they no longer feel. Send for some women who still have

67

the ability to feel and cry so that they might wail against what the devil is doing."

Get a picture of what these mourning women were to do. They were to weep and wail, to mourn in sackcloth and ashes, as a sign to wake up everybody around them to face the fact that the devil was destroying them and that death was on the way. They were God's warning system to God's people. They were the alarm system, the tornado signal, the air-raid siren. They were the ones God was going to use to warn His people of the impending consequences of sin. They were the ones who created a platform from which the words of Jeremiah could ring forth with stinging conviction.

These were women who had a God-given destiny to destroy the power of Satan over God's people by waking up God's children and calling them to a mourning of repentance. These were women who were instructed to teach their daughters to weep against sin and the assault of the devil.

God has a destiny for women today. He wants His women loosed to open their mouths and cry out against the evil that the devil has put upon God's people.

You have ideas that haven't been voiced.

You have energy that hasn't been released.

You have abilities that haven't been used.

You have power that hasn't been loosed.

You have spiritual gifts that haven't been given expression.

The day has come for you to forget those things which are past and look toward the future. It's time to look at what you *can* be

and what *you* can do

and what you *can* say

and what you *can* possess that will bring glory to God and cause the devil to be defeated and your destiny to be fulfilled.

The devil tried to take you out. Oh, time and again he's tried to take you out. But God let you go through everything you've been through so you might come to the place of crying out against that particular evil and in the process of crying out, bruise the head of the devil. God expects you to open up and give birth to the treasure in you so that you can turn the tables on the devil that the devil *thought* he had turned on you!

Were you abused as a child? God wants you to cry out against that abuse. He has put something in you that you can use to crush the abusing head of Satan BRING IT FORTH!

Were you raped by a boyfriend who said he loved you but only wanted to use you? God wants you to cry out against rape. He has put something in you that you can use to crush the raping head of Satan. BRING IT FORTH.

Were you pushed into a prison of failure as a child so that you became so afraid to take any risks that you have spent a lifetime cowered before other people until you became a doormat for society? God wants you to cry out against fear and failure and the loss of self-respect. He has put something in you that you can use to crush the lying, fear-causing head of Satan. BRING IT FORTH.

I don't know what it is that God intends for you to use in defeating the devil. It may be a new business. It may be a new ministry. It may be a job in a certain area. It may be

69

a volunteer position that you are to fill. I don't know what it is specifically that you have within you or what opportunity He has given you, but I know that God has something in you and an opportunity for you. USE IT! The devil can't stand up against what God has given to you.

Is there an idea that you've had for years but have never acted upon?

Is there a dream you've held but have been afraid to voice?

Is there a drive that you feel welling up in you from time to time, but one that you've never put into full motion?

Is there an opportunity that you see but you've been afraid to reach out and grab hold of it?

It's time for you to BRING FORTH the treasure that God has given you.

So many women have spent years, even decades, locked up in a prison of worry over what people will say about them. The result is that they have failed to give birth to those things that they could have done, and would have done, and should have done. NOW IS THE TIME! Yes, *today* is your day.

The time has come for the birthing
of the treasure God has put in you.

Part II

Loosed From Past Failures

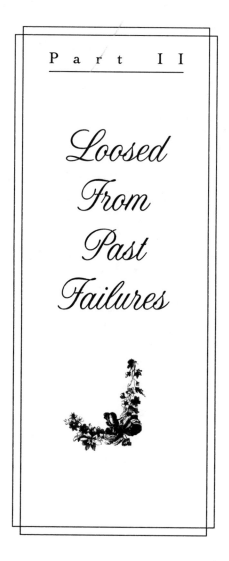

∽ A Fallen Woman ∼

Eve was not only the first woman and the mother of all living. She is representative of many other firsts as well —

the first marriage,

the first family,

the first marital conflict,

the first offering,

the first murder,

the first family division,

and the first rekindling of a woman's dream.

We often think of Eve as being a "fallen woman" — she fell for the devil's temptation and with Adam, became the cause of the "fall" of all mankind. Because of Eve, every woman and man today is born in a fallen spiritual state and needs to be born again spiritually.

What we need to recognize is that God had a plan of redemption for Eve. He had an appointed seed for her to bear for His purposes.

73

From the Scriptures:

And Adam knew his wife again; and she bare a son, and called his name Seth: For God, said she, hath appointed me another seed instead of Abel, whom Cain slew.

And to Seth, to him also there was born a son; and he called his name Enos: then began men to call upon the name of the LORD.

— Genesis 4:25–26

∽ Twelve ∽

You Were Created for Wholeness and Life

Eve . . .

the mother

of all living.

— Genesis 3:20

Eve was created in the man . . . called out of the man . . . and then presented to the man.

She was called woman, bone of his bone, flesh of his flesh, created to stand beside man to help meet his need, to help make up the difference. Together, Eve and Adam, woman and man, are a picture of the wholeness of God.

Have you heard the dispute that has been raised in recent years about whether God is male or female? Some people are seeking to change the Bible to have either neutral terms for God or to use the pronoun "She" as often as the pronoun "He" to refer to God.

On the one hand, I believe these people are onto something, in that we have been chauvinistic at times in describing God in only male terms, often to the degree that many women have felt excluded from relating to God. But on the other hand, we must understand that sexuality is related to our physical composition. And God is a Spirit.

75

When it comes to spiritual issues, there is neither male nor female, Greek nor Jew, bond nor free. We are all one in the anointing in Christ Jesus.

God is our Father. Jesus referred to Him that way. He manifests Himself to us as Father. But God also said that He is El Shaddai, which literally means "The Breasted One." He said, "As a mother nourishes her child, so I will nourish you." He said to His children, "I am full of whatever it is that you are crying for, My child." As much as God is the epitome of fatherhood in His provision and defense of His children, so He is also the epitome of motherhood in His nurture and love.

The only way we can begin to picture the sexual identity of God is to look at Adam before he was divided from Eve. The Bible tells us that at creation, God said, "Let us make man in our image, after our likeness: and let them have dominion. . . . So God created man in his own image, in the image of God created he him; male and female created he them" (Genesis 1:26–27).

Eve, the woman, was hidden in the "womb" of man. When Adam got to the place where he needed someone, God did not need to reenter the creative process. He simply said, "Adam, I'm going to put you to sleep and pull out of you what I've already created in you. I've already made exactly what it is that you need."

Adam had absolutely no trouble in relating to Eve because she was him. When they came together, they were a picture of total godliness. They were one flesh, a mirror of one God.

When men and women come together today in the Spirit, they too are a total picture of all the characteristics of God. That is one of the reasons that the enemy wants to do everything he can to divide men and women; that is why he has declared war on our marriages. He knows that when we are separated, we do not give a total picture of godliness to the world.

Neither man nor woman can totally depict God's nature without the other. We men need the gentleness, tenderness, femininity, love, mercy, and compassion of women. Women need men to express the strength, provision, power, protection, and defense of God. When we come together, we are able to express the total nature of God to a hurting world. And the devil doesn't want to see that happen.

Anything the devil can do to divide us and make us suspicious and wary of each other, he'll do it. If it isn't wife abuse, it's male bashing. He delights in bitter, angry mothers who teach their daughters to hate men and to live individualistic lives. Just because mama had a conflict with her husband, doesn't mean you have to have a conflict with yours!

When men and women come together, God allows them to act out who He is — they are privileged to be partners with Him in the creative process of life. And the celebration of the union of man and woman is children ... life. Just as God breathed His life into Adam, so we are allowed to breathe life into this world through the bearing of children.

77

You were created as a woman for a very special purpose — first, to experience wholeness and union, and then, to bear children. That dual purpose is not limited to the natural. It is a supernatural purpose. God created you to become the mother of something spiritual that will live forever!

Trust God today to make you whole and to use you to bear His life in the world.

~ *Thirteen* ~

Shut the Door!

If she be a door, we will

inclose her with

boards of cedar.

— Song of Solomon 8:9

No sooner had God created Eve than the devil sought her out to talk to her. Why? Because he knew something about Eve, just as he knows something about women today. He knows that women are the door to life.

Women are the only legal entry into the earth realm. If it is going to be born, it is going to be born of a woman. If it is going to come from the eternal realm into the realm of time, it is going to come through the door of a woman's womb. The devil is waiting at the door.

Most women don't seem to understand that they are the passageway — the entry for life. It is an awesome responsibility, an awesome privilege.

We each were chosen by God from the foundations of eternity, but in order to get us from eternity into time, God has only one method — that we be born of a woman. God is so serious about this law of His creation that when He got ready to pour Himself into human flesh and live on

79

this earth, He didn't violate His own method but rather, was born of a woman.

It is this fact that puts women on the devil's hit list. The enemy is opposed to life. He deals in sickness, destruction, denial, devastation, thievery, and death. The enemy knows that if he is going to be successful, he must conquer the legal entryway to life.

Woman, guard your doors and lock them. Slam your fence gates shut and chain them tight. Be very careful what you let come through you . . .

what you let affect you . . .

what you let influence you . . .

and be careful what spirit you let

loose in your mind . . .

in your emotion . . .

in your family.

Shut the door!

Shut the door on that confusion.

Shut the door on that depression.

Shut the door on that temptation.

Shut the door on that evil spirit.

You are shutting the door in the devil's face.

Solomon wrote in the Song of Solomon, "We have a little sister, and she hath no breasts . . . If she be a wall, we will build upon her a palace of silver: and if she be a door, we will inclose her with boards of cedar" (Song of Solomon 8:8–9).

Solomon was describing a sister who was immature. He said if she was found to be "swinging loose," he would teach her how to "keep herself." He would close her in so she didn't give entrance to just any old thing or any old person that happened to come along. But if she proved to be a wall — if she was found to be solid in what she believed and how she behaved — then he would build on her.

This is the stance we need to take in the church. If we have a woman in our midst who is a little "loose," we need to surround her with strong women of faith, rather than gossip about her or shun her. We need to teach her how to keep herself, how not to put herself into vulnerable positions, how not to be "shopping" for a man every time she meets one.

So many women have been abused, and abused women don't know anything about how to have a healthy relationship with a man. Their concept of men has been shattered. They don't know about brotherly love. We need to teach them about the type of love that can exist between men and women that is not sexual — the types of love that can be brotherly and comforting and friendly. It is important that we heal the concept of family in the church, and it begins with our teaching one another what it means to keep oneself pure and to relate in ways that are right before God.

Guard the door of your life, your soul, your spirit. Shut the door on the devil today!

You have precious treasure inside you that needs protecting. You have the capacity to bear life. Don't let the enemy steal it from you.

81

Slam the door on the devil today. Give entrance only to the Holy Spirit and open yourself up only to those things that are from God.

 *Fourteen*

Stand in His Strength

God is able

to make [us] stand.

— Romans 14:4

The enemy confronted Eve in the garden. He wanted to be in the family. He wanted to get in the door of her life, in her relationship with her husband, and in her relationship with God. He wanted to gain authority over the earth realm and to be the god of this world, and in order to do so, he knew he had to have influence over the one who held the key to producing life.

The enemy said to Eve, "Girl, take a look at this fruit." And Eve did. She looked, she touched, she ate. She became a partaker in something that God had said not to do.

Now, I don't fully blame Eve for the consequences of what happened as a result of her disobedience. What Eve did still could have been salvaged, but when Adam joined Eve in disobedience, destruction was assured. Adam missed his opportunity to become a full picture of the "last Adam," Jesus Christ.

Adam, in his weakness of need, died with his bride.

Jesus, in His strength of love, died for His bride.

83

Every child that was born to Adam and Eve was born after Adam and Eve had sinned. Every child born to them was therefore fallen, shaped in iniquity. When the Bible says that we are all born in sin, the word is *sin*, not sins. We are born with a sin nature, the state of sin, not as the result of a sinful act or with a host of sins attributed to our account.

I am very weary of two kinds of people — those who brag about their old sinful nature, and those who act as if they never had one.

Some people seem to boast about what they did before they accepted Jesus Christ as their Savior. It's as if they are working for bragging rights — they seem to enjoy recounting all the details about how bad they were.

The fact is, it doesn't matter what you did before you were saved or how bad your life was. It doesn't matter how bad your sins were or how many of them you committed. God didn't save you because you had accumulated a long list of sinful deeds. He saved you because He loved you and He wanted to change your sin nature — the nature in you that is prone to disobey God. We were all born with identically the same sin nature. We inherited it from our first parents, Adam and Eve.

There are other people who act as if they were born lily white. Let me assure you that if the Lord hadn't saved you when He did, you could have done anything . . .

run with anyone . . .

been anything . . .

or even died as the result of anything that any other person has ever experienced in the sin department.

The fact that you didn't engage in more sinful acts before God reached down and lifted you up is a miracle of God!

If the truth was known, if God hadn't taken hold of us when He did we all would have committed horrible sinful acts, and more of them than we could recount. We may not have done all the bad things that we had the capacity or desire to do before we were saved, but if we hadn't been saved when we were, we probably would have done them!

There are probably some things frustrating you today that are things you didn't "get to do" before you got saved. I know many people who wrestle with those things daily. They still have a desire to sin, which is part of their flesh nature, even after they have been saved.

After a major earthquake, tremors can continue for hours, days, even weeks. They are called "aftershocks." The same is true in the spirit realm. After a person is saved, she can still have tremors of temptation from her former life.

Believe me when I tell you, those who don't tell you about their sins or who don't seem to have sinned very much . . . have thought about sinning! We all have thought about doing some bad things that we haven't actually done.

If we are born with the weakness of Eve and Adam, what are we to do when the devil comes along?

The Bible says, "Having done all . . . Stand therefore" (Ephesians 6:13–14). And in Romans 14:4 we read, "God is able to make [us] stand." Not in your strength but in the strength of Jesus Christ. You can't stand on your strength. By yourself, you are just another Eve. But in the strength of Jesus, you can stand and not give in.

about how we are to live our
lives . . .

> every time we start feeling
> pity that we didn't receive
> everything we needed as a
> child.

Some days we need a little more strength than on other days. But every time we need strength, we are to run to the Breasted One. He has what it is that we need. He longs to hold us and comfort us and impart to us the strength we need to move forward in our lives. Draw from Him the strength you need to stand.

My wife breast-fed our first daughter. I didn't know anything about what it meant to breast-feed a baby. They told us in the classes that we attended that this was nature's way and the best method for both a mother and baby. I said to my wife, "Let's do it." Seemed good to me!

86

My wife tried it. And it didn't take long before we found ourselves asking, "How can something so natural be so hard?" The baby didn't seem to know that breast-feeding was natural. She didn't seem to be able to get enough milk and she cried and screamed around the clock. Finally I got a bottle and said, "Here! We're going to try a new method!"

God's way isn't always easy. It may be the perfect way, the ideal way, the truly "natural" way according to God's creation . . . but you still may need to work at it. Just because something is right doesn't mean it's easy.

We often have to work at drawing from God what it is that we need.

The tremors of temptation, the moods and attitudes toward sin, will pass if you will only stand up to them in His name. The blood of Jesus Christ has set you free and will continue to uphold you, if you will just stand. On Christ the solid rock we STAND!

Announce to the devil that when he comes around with his temptations, you are going to stand in Christ. You are going to stand until the shaking quits . . .

until the thunder stops rolling . . .

until midnight passes into dawn . . .

until you feel peace again . . .

until the wave of loneliness

passes . . .

until your marriage is

restored . . .

until you come

out of debt . . .

until your

struggle

is over!

87

When we do the standing, God does the strengthening. Paul said, "I can do all things through Christ which strengtheneth me" (Philippians 4:13).

Christ doesn't just strengthen us once. He strengthens us again and again and again. He strengthens us every time we face a difficult challenge . . .

every time a memory comes up to haunt us . . .

every time we are reminded of our

imperfect past . . .

every time we face a decision

Drawing from God the strength you need to stand up to the devil may take effort. It may take your praise, your prayer, your getting into His Word with an intensity you've never had before.

But the fact is, you can stand if you want to stand.

Choose to stand up to the devil today

in the strength of Christ Jesus.

∾ Fifteen ∽

Refuse to Be Killed

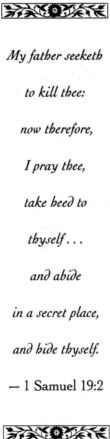

My father seeketh

to kill thee:

now therefore,

I pray thee,

take heed to

thyself . . .

and abide

in a secret place,

and hide thyself.

— 1 Samuel 19:2

Adam and Eve were created in the likeness of God but all of their children were born in their likeness — in the likeness of sin. Their children were born dysfunctional.

We are all from dysfunctional families. I get amused when I watch talk shows on which they have flown in a person who has a terrible story to tell. The person is veiled behind a curtain so you only see her silhouette as she says, "I came from a dysfunctional family." People in the audience ask, "How did you feel? What was it like to grow up in a dysfunctional family? Were you emotionally upset?"

I want to say, "Ah, come on. Get out of here! Why are you asking all those questions as if you don't know the answer from your own life?" Everybody I know or ever hope to meet came from a dysfunctional family. Every family on earth has something wrong with it that keeps it from being perfect. The first family was dysfunctional and every family since then has been dysfunctional.

Quit feeling sorry for yourself because you came from a dysfunctional family. So did every other person. Quit allowing the enemy to make you feel guilty as if your problem is some kind of special case. All people were born with problems regardless of their color, race, educational background, the part of town they lived in, the type of parents they had, or the things they went through.

Every person is born inwardly depraved, regardless of how that depravity might be expressed. In the case of Cain, the firstborn son of Adam and Eve, depravity was expressed as hatred, jealousy, and murder. The first child ever born was a murderer. The first family on earth was marked by crime. The first person murdered was a son.

90

Families today are marked by murder, including the family of God, the church. In fact, you haven't really been killed until you've been killed by a brother or sister in the church! I know some women who made it through the worst possible life on the streets only to be driven half crazy by saints.

It's time we say to those in our family — both our natural family and our spiritual family — "I love you, I'm related to you, I care about you . . . but I won't let you kill me."

You had better adopt that attitude toward every person in your life, including your husband, your children, your friends, your boss, the people you work with, the members of your church. You need to say to them, "Jesus died for me. That's all the dying that needs to be done. I'm not going to let you kill me. I'm going to hide myself in Him. I won't let you kill me."

I'm not talking about the body. I'm talking about your resisting those who will attempt to kill something in your spirit and soul. I'm talking about people who will come at you to try to kill something in your emotions, your attitude, your inner life. They'll try to get you to sin with them, or to give into the temptation you feel to sin.

They'll say to you, "It's alright. It won't matter if you do this just this once. It's just a little thing, a one-time deal."

Others might say to you, "Nothing is going to get better. You might as well give up and sit down in your ashes because nothing is ever going to change and nothing is ever going to be right in your life."

No! Those who will say such things to you are agents of death itself creeping up on you and coming at you in disguise. Don't let them kill you! Stand up to them in the strength of Jesus Christ and say, "I'm not going to let you drive me crazy with your lies and your temptations. I'm not going to let you lead me into sin. I refuse to let you kill in me what God has birthed in me!"

91

Get your praise out. Start praising God for what He has done for you. Celebrate the life He has given you. Declare to God and to every person who talks death to you — "My life isn't over. There's still more that God has for me to do and to say and to be. I'm choosing life. I refuse to go back down that road of death."

Say no to those drugs . . .

say no to that sinful relationship . . .

say no to that evil desire . . .

say no to those thoughts of
depression and suicide . . .

say no to that thing or that person who is
trying to lead you straight back to a life of dying instead
of living. Don't let yourself be killed!

Stand strong in Christ today. Refuse to
let the depravity of another person
pull you down or destroy you.

92

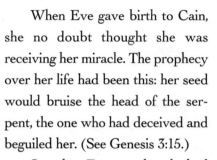

Dealing With Your Cains and Abels

Cain rose up against Abel his brother, and slew him. . . . And Cain went out from the presence of the LORD, and dwelt in the land of Nod, on the east of Eden.

— Genesis 4:8, 16

When Eve gave birth to Cain, she no doubt thought she was receiving her miracle. The prophecy over her life had been this: her seed would bruise the head of the serpent, the one who had deceived and beguiled her. (See Genesis 3:15.)

So, when Eve saw that she had given birth to a son, she probably said, "Here it is! This is my miracle. This is what God promised. Here is my savior, the one who is going to straighten out this mess that I created, the one who is going to undo what I have done."

Then when she gave birth to Abel, she no doubt said, "Why, here's another miracle — another opportunity to defeat the serpent. One of these two has got to be the Messiah! Surely one of these boys is God's answer."

93

But things didn't turn out the way Eve had hoped. In fact, things didn't turn out right at all.

Have you ever raised someone who didn't turn out right? When a woman raises a child who falls into sin and gets into trouble, she feels responsible. She feels as if their outcome is her fault.

Eve probably had an idea early in their lives how Cain and Abel might turn out. The rebellious, quick-tempered, proud, easily-upset Cain didn't get that way overnight. He didn't develop his strong work ethic and his drive to achieve success in a day. His violent streak didn't appear suddenly.

Likewise, Abel's desire to please, his humility, his obedience, his nurturing and "tending" traits weren't the product of spontaneous combustion.

I suspect that Abel was always Eve's favorite. We see mothers everywhere who say, "Oh, Abel's making good grades. Abel's on his way to college. Abel always does what I tell him to do. Abel does the nicest things for me. Now I'm praying for Cain, but Abel is doing just fine." In every family, there always seems to be a Cain and an Abel.

The day came, however, when Cain killed Abel. The first woman, who had become the first wife, and who was the first mother, now attended the first funeral. She had lost her baby son. She knew the pain — a pain like no other pain — of lowering the body of her beloved child into the ground.

Not only that, but her elder son was as good as dead — marked for destruction and living on the run. Cain was alive, but he was dead as far as she was concerned. He wasn't there for her either.

There is one kind of pain that we experience when we lose something we thought we would always have. There is another kind of pain in having something that you are perpetually in the state of losing. Cain represents that second kind of pain for Eve. He is alive, but he isn't. He survived, but he didn't. There is no loneliness like that of feeling alone even if you aren't alone.

I hear so many single women say, "I want to be married." They sing the praises of marriage with a high-C pitch. They think that if they just get married their loneliness in life will be solved.

They don't seem to know that there are many married women who are still waiting to be "married." They don't know that there are tens of thousands of women who get up every morning and fight loneliness all through the day because they are linked to someone who isn't there. Now, their husbands may be snoring in the bed next to them. Their husbands may be sitting at the breakfast table. But they aren't there. They are present physically, but they are absent emotionally and spiritually. It's terrible to be with somebody and still be by yourself. It's far worse than the loneliness of not being with anybody at all.

Many relationships don't work, but they persist. The people in them exist, but they don't live. They are dying on the inside, even if they show all the signs of living on the outside.

Cain represents all those relationships in which a person is there, but you can't trust him or depend on him.

95

Cain was not dead, but he was as good as dead. He was a member of the "living dead."

Eve couldn't stop grieving for Cain because his life wasn't over. She couldn't pronounce a final benediction on Cain because he was in a lingering limbo. At least she could have a funeral for Abel.

So many women I know today have "Cains" in their lives. They have unresolved issues, which is what Cain was to Eve. They have relationships that are like sustained notes — there is no melody, but there also is no ending, no conclusion, no resolution. They are unable to determine in their minds if something is over or still in process. They feel as if they are on hold. They don't know where they are at, or where things are going. One day things seem to be moving in one direction, and the next day things seem to be going the opposite way. Unless a woman learns to deal with the Cain in her life, she is in danger of cracking up.

We mourn for what we lose. But at the same time, we know where the thing that we lost is located. We know where the body has been laid. We know where the tombstone has been placed.

But in cases of Cain, there is no body, no funeral, no grave, no tombstone. You just don't know where he is. Now you see him, now you don't.

It's hard to praise if there's a Cain in your life because you don't know what it is that you should be praising God for. The reason you don't know is because you don't know where he's at, and until you know where he's at, you can't know where you're at. If you don't know where you're at, you're confused. And those who are confused find it difficult to get beyond their confusion to see the absolutes and the sovereignty of God.

If you are going to be able to receive your next blessing . . .

if you are going to be in a position to experience the next move of God in your life . . .

if you are going to come out of the valley of the shadow of death . . .

you have got to let your past go.

You have got to bury Abel.

You have got to say "goodbye" to Cain. Otherwise you will never be able to say "hello" to what God has for you next.

You can't continue to pine away over somebody you were in love with fifteen years ago — somebody who has been married for ten years and is out roasting wieners in the park with his family while you are at home crying in your soup. You've got to let that person go from your heart and your mind. If you don't, you won't be able to say "hello" to the right man God brings your way.

When Jesus said to let the dead bury their dead, He was saying that we shouldn't be overly concerned with that which is over. (See Matthew 8:22.) We should let what is over be over.

You wouldn't let a dead man hold onto you. Why let a dead relationship keep you in its grasp? Why let yesterday pull you down and hold you back?

Today is the day to say "goodbye" to what you've lost — both to what you may have buried and to what has

97

gone away from you. It is your day to stop grieving and go forward.

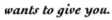

*Ask God to help you deal with your
disappointment and loss so you can be
ready for the blessing He still
wants to give you.*

Seventeen

Let Go
of Your Past

When I became a man,

I put away

childish things.

— 1 Corinthians 13:11

Eve woke up a wife. Can you imagine? On her first day on planet earth she may have heard her husband ask, "Honey, where are my socks?"

She had no training for the job, no preparation — it was a matter of "well, that's the way it is." It's very difficult to do something that you've never seen done before. It's difficult to be something if you've never seen it modeled for you. It's very tough to be a good wife if you never saw a good wife in action. No wonder Eve went for a walk in the garden. She was probably stressed out!

Eve was created without a childhood, without having had an opportunity to be a little girl. She stepped right into being a wife, and then a mother. She was a woman before she had a chance to be a girl.

Now in Eve's case, that may have been alright. God had a plan and He did things His way. But in our world today, there are lots of women who found themselves

99

being women before they had a chance to be girls. They didn't have an opportunity to know what it meant to be innocent, to feel free to trust, or what it meant to receive genuine love.

Sometimes life can come at us too fast. Sometimes we have our childhoods stripped away from us. The little girl in you may never have had an opportunity to be a little girl. And if that happened, you were robbed of something very precious.

I tell my daughters, "Be little girls as long as you can." I look around sometimes and I can't believe what I see — mothers who have dressed up their little girls to look like women, with their hair all done up and earrings in their ears and lipstick on their mouths . . . even at four months old!

I want my daughters to be innocent and free and trusting of others as long as possible.

Whether you had a girlhood or not, you must not use the past as your excuse. You must refuse to blame your past for your present and future.

The fact is . . .

You can never relive your past.

You can't go back and make it different.

You are not the person you were then and you are never going to be that person again.

You can't go back into your mother's womb.

You can't relive your first marriage.

Your past is your past.

It is over!

Accept that fact and dismiss your past and move on. Let it go!

Let go of anything that is holding you back,

or slowing you down,

and keeping you all

bound up inside.

If you are holding onto your past, it's because there is something about your past that you think you still need.

I feel certain that if I needed my baby clothes, my mother could go up in her attic and find them. Up in that attic somewhere, she has my pacifier. I know she has my size-30 gym shorts from junior high. She has boxes and bags and bundles of things in her attic "just in case we ever need them."

My mother seems to have the mind-set that if we ever fall on hard times and are on skid row, she can go up in her attic and find something that will get us through. I tease her, "What are you going to do? Sew all my baby clothes into a quilt to keep us warm?"

When I go to visit her, she often pulls out something that she found. She'll say to me, "I've got a copy of your first check, the one you got for cutting grass when you were nine years old. Do you want to see it?" I say, "No." And she'll show it to me anyway. She has kept all kinds of stuff over the years.

I know my mother isn't the only woman who has done this. When I speak to women's groups, I often ask them, "How many of you hold onto stuff from the past?" Just about every woman in the room looks guilty.

When my wife was expecting our first child, she was given all kinds of stuff from people who stopped by the house, saying, "Here's this, here's that — just in case you

101

need it." They'd tell her how their baby or their grand-baby had used the items, or how they themselves had worn the item as a child. I said to my wife, "They aren't blessing us. They're cleaning out their closets!" We had stacks and stacks of stuff for our baby daughter, including a whole stack of little boy clothes!

My wife has this tendency, too. After each pregnancy, she wanted to keep her maternity clothes, just in case she might need them again. After our last baby, I said, "Throw them away!"

As a man, I don't understand that tendency. As far as I am concerned, when you hold onto things like that, they keep you tied to the past.

Have you ever noticed that when you visit old people, they spend most of their time talking about the past? They'll say to you, "Do you remember the time? Do you recall how we used to . . . ?" They want to relive those times. I suspect that it's because they think those were the best times of their lives and they aren't expecting anything better ever to come along. There is something about the past that they need in order to give meaning to their present.

People who don't let go of things easily, have little faith. They cling to things because they fear they will never be able to replace them. They won't give you the last twenty-dollar bill they have in their purse or pocket because they fear they won't ever have another one.

Don't you know that God has more for you? He has something else for you. If you are trusting God for your future, then you have not yet seen your best days. There's more before you than there is behind you.

It doesn't matter how young you are, or how old you are. If you are alive today, then God has kept you here for this very hour and He has something more for you.

He has something more for you to be . . .
something more for you to say . . .
    something more for you to do . . .
        something more for you to
        experience . . .
            something more for you to praise.

You are alive today because God still has a reason for you to be alive.

I want you to get it into your heart, in your mind, in your spirit . . . there's a reason for you to go forward. You may have lost the Garden of Eden, you may have buried your Abel, you may have lost your Cain . . . but God has something ahead for your future. He has something good planned for you. You aren't dead. You're alive . . . so LIVE!

103

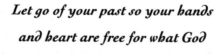

Let go of your past so your hands
and heart are free for what God
has for you NOW.

~ *Eighteen* ~

There's More Life Ahead

> *I had fainted, unless I had believed to see the goodness of the LORD in the land of the living.*
>
> — Psalm 27:13

104

I have no doubt that Eve was the first person who knew what it meant to feel depressed. Her hopes had been dashed. She had experienced murder in her family. She had lost both of her sons — one to death, the other to a curse. She felt the failure of having produced an outlaw from her own womb. She no doubt felt regret that she had ever become pregnant in the first place.

Regret is something that many women need to face today. There can be no recovery until a woman is willing to look at herself in the mirror and say, "I messed up." People who blame other people never recover because they live in a state of denial. Any time you blame another person for your problem, you put that person in control of your life. You are saying with your blame, "I can't get out until you let me out. I can't succeed until you allow me to succeed.

I can't move forward in my life until you give me the green light." That's a lie of the devil!

You must accept responsibility for your own actions. You may not have done it all, but you contributed. It may not be all your fault, but you need to accept responsibility for the part that was yours. You must be able to say to yourself, "I wasn't without fault. I was a contributing factor."

Unless you are able to accept responsibility for your actions, you will be eaten up with unresolved guilt in your life. It will rot inside you and erupt in your life in the form of jealousy and anger and hatred and bitterness. Find the Cains in your life and deal with them. Confront the issues. Challenge the lies that the devil will try to speak in your mind, when he tells you, "It's not your fault. It's all his fault. You were right, he was wrong. Things were just out of control. You didn't do anything bad. Somebody else is to blame for all this." No! Accept your share of the responsibility for what has gone wrong and ask God to forgive you.

105

God is too wise and too loving to put your destiny into the hands of another person. He doesn't trust the actions of another person to control your future. What you do from this point on in your life is up to you. How you feel and how you react and what you do and what you say and what you choose and how you deal with the past is solely your responsibility. It's your decision.

If you will face up to your own sin and take hold of the hand of our forgiving God, you can overcome anything. You can overcome the past influence of any person . . . the evil of any circumstance . . . and live and not die!

You don't need to live with depression,

oppression,

or suppression. God wants you
to come out of your feelings of failure and rejection and
regret, and start living!

A number of years ago I went through a time of great
depression in my life. I'd preach and then go back to my
room, sit on the floor with the lights out, and cry in the
dark. Nothing was wrong, but everything was wrong.

I didn't care what I did or what others did to me. I
didn't care if I got up in the morning. I didn't care what I
wore or what I looked like. I didn't care what other people thought of me because I didn't have any thoughts for
anything but the way I felt. And I felt so low that I didn't
care if I lived or died. When people were around, I'd smile
and praise the Lord. But when I was alone, I'd go back
into the dark and cry.

I preached a lot about heaven because that's where I
wanted to go. I read about heaven and studied the Scriptures about heaven and wrote songs about heaven
because that's the only place I wanted to be. I didn't want
to be here on this earth. I wanted out.

That time in my life was before my ministry began to
flourish, before I wrote any books, before I started speaking across the nation. There were many things that I had
already overcome at that point in my life, but there were
still many things that I had to face. I was so overwhelmed
by discouragement that for months, I wanted to die.

I asked the Lord, "What's wrong with me? What is
happening to me?"

He said, "Son, your heart has fainted. You've been through so much that your heart — not your physical heart, but your emotional and spiritual heart — has fainted."

I said, "What shall I do?"

He said, "Wait on Me. Be of good courage. I'm going to strengthen your heart."

Let me tell you something about the way things work. Just before you birth that new seed, just before you see your miracle, just before your promise is fulfilled . . . that's the time when all hell seems to break out against you.

Just before you come into your purpose, that's when others will do their best to nail you to the tree.

Just before you experience the fullness of God's power working in you, that's the time when the devil will try to break you.

Just before the baby arrives, that's when the labor pains reach their peak.

All the while, however, you have all the symptoms of a miracle growing in you.

Before I ever wrote a book, I wrote a letter to myself. I said to myself, "Don't die. Don't die. It's going to get better in a minute."

I told myself, "You can make it. You can make it. Don't give up."

I said, "You have gone through too much to die now. You may cry, but don't die. There's got to be something else for you. There's got to be a reason for you to feel the way you feel. There's got to be a blessing that is better than anything you have ever felt before."

107

Those are the very words I believe the Lord wants me to say to you.

Don't die.

Don't die.

Don't die.

Keep standing.

Keep standing.

Keep standing.

God is about to give you another seed to birth. He's about to open up the windows of heaven to you and pour you out a blessing that will be so great you won't even have room enough to receive it all.

I can't tell you what day I came out of my depression. When God restores you, He does so in a way that suddenly you are walking in the light and you can hardly recall how dark your life had been.

I suspect it was just that way for Eve. When she held Seth in her arms, her thoughts of Abel faded. Her burden about Cain lifted. She had another miracle, another opportunity.

When you move into the fullness of your appointment with God's destiny for you, you won't think any more about those things that are in your past. You won't have time — you won't have the inclination — to dwell on your failures, your mistakes, your former life. You will be so busy raising up your miracle and living in your blessing that all the former things in your life will be not only out of your sight and out of your mind, but out of your heart.

You will be free. You will be loosed at last to do and be what it is that God has appointed you to do and to be!

Don't quit or give up.
Give birth to that promise that
God has put in your life.
Look for it to be born in you
and to be a blessing!

109

∽ *Nineteen* ∼

Your Appointed Seed

God, said she,

hath appointed me

another seed

instead of Abel.

— Genesis 4:25

You have a predetermined appointment with God that has been set from the foundations of the earth, and that appointment isn't over until God says it's over. You may think that all of your good days are in the past, but the very fact that you are alive says that God wants you to be alive. He is not through with you yet. You have an appointment.

The angels of the Lord are going to keep you here as long as God wants you here.

No weapon formed against you is going to prosper as long as God wants you here.

Your appointment isn't over until God says it's over!

Even after all she had been through with Cain and Abel, Eve still had an appointment with God. In spite of all that she had experienced, all the heartache and hard times she had known, she had an appointed task. Eve said, "God has appointed me another seed." (See Genesis 4:25.) Her appointment involved having another baby, another son. She named him Seth.

God has another promise with your name on it today. He has appointed you another seed.

In spite of all that you've been through,

> all that you've suffered,
>
> all of your tears,
>
> all of your failures and mistakes,
>
> all of your misjudgment and mismanagement,
>
> all that you've lost,
>
> all that has left you . . .

> God has another "baby" for you to birth.

Don't give up.

Don't give in.

Don't give way.

God has another method to bring you the blessing He has destined for you to receive.

When you make an appointment, you set a date and a time in the present for something that is going to happen in the future. And that's exactly what God has done in setting His appointment with you.

God's destiny for you is preset. He has known all along that you would go through what you've been through to get to the place where you are right now. Even so, He still has an appointment with you. He has not cancelled out. There's still something on His calendar that has your name on it.

The devil knew that God had a plan for you. That's why he worked so hard to wipe you out. He didn't want you to live long enough to keep your full appointment, to live out all that God had in store for you. He knew there was more ahead. He knew it was good. He knew it had to

111

do with life. That's why he tried so hard to deal you a death-blow early on.

He sent trials . . .

troubles . . .

and tribulations to destroy you — and if you refused to be destroyed on the outside, he tried even harder to destroy you on the inside.

Start looking ahead. There's something coming up on God's calendar and it's got your name on it. There's something good just over the horizon of tomorrow that's for your life,

your marriage,

your family,

your work,

your ministry.

For everything that you have lost in your life . . . God has another seed.

For everything that you loved and that died . . . God has another seed.

For everything that you lost and can no longer hold . . . God has another seed.

Every time the devil tells you that you are going down, that you are going to die, that you are going to cave in, that there's nothing else for you, tell him, "You are a liar. There's got to be something else. I have an appointment with God. He has another seed for me to birth. He has another miracle for me to hold."

God has called you with an eternal purpose. Where you are right now is not where you are going. He still has an appointed task for you to finish.

God still has an appointed seed

for you to birth.

ᔟ Twenty ᔟ

Keep Your Appointment

Then began men to

call upon the

name of the LORD.

— Genesis 4:26

114

It seems that every time I get ready for a major appointment, something comes up to try to slow me down. People will call and just want to chit-chat. I'll be pacing the floor trying to find a way to get off the phone, but the person will just go on and on.

Problems always seem to come up. The car keys won't be anywhere in sight. The gas gauge will read empty. Traffic will be heavy. An accident will block the highway. It seems everything possible will arise to slow me down.

When God has an appointed seed for you to birth, there may be obstacles you have to hurdle. There may be delays you have to endure. There may be things you have to refuse.

When God appoints a task for you, there's no time for idle talk. There's no time for gossip. In order for you to receive what God has for you, you are going to have to hang up on some folk . . .

you are going to have to hang up on some situations . . .

you are going to have to outlast or outmaneuver some circumstances . . .

you are going to have to say "no" to
some activities that will pull you
away from your appointment or
delay you from keeping it.
You will have no time for foolishness,
pity parties,
or side shows.

If you are going to hold onto your miracle, your dream, the fulfillment of God's plan for your life, then you are going to have to keep moving, keep moving, keep moving. Always keep moving toward what God has for you.

You may have to crawl to get there, but keep crawling.

You may have to cry a lot of tears along the way, but keep walking.

You may get knocked down, but get up and keep going.

Don't let anything keep you from keeping your appointment!

The thing that God has for you must be done. That's the way God feels about His plan for you. Write yourself a note, "I have an appointment. It must be kept."

Eve kept her appointment. She had a son named Seth and he had a son named Enos. The Bible says that it was with the birth of Enos that Eve's descendants began to "call upon the name of the Lord." That means that they began to trust God with their lives and to identify completely with Him. Seth was God's man. Enos was God's man. The people of Enos were God's people.

Eve lived to see her son and her grandson walk in holiness before the Lord. She lived to see her miracle. She lived to see her son and her grandson turn back to God

115

and live in obedience, reversing the tide of disobedience and reversing the curse on her family.

There's a reversal ahead for you, too, if you will only keep your appointment with God.

Don't let anything keep you from your
appointment with God today.

116

Part III

Loosed
to Express
Emotions

✧ A Crying Woman ✧

Hannah was deeply distressed over her failure to bear a child. She was the wife of Elkanah, who was also married to Peninnah. Peninnah had children and in her jealousy at Elkanah's great love for Hannah, she ridiculed and provoked Hannah because she was childless. In a word, Peninnah made Hannah's life miserable.

Hannah took her grief to the door of the tabernacle, the closest she could go to the holy of holies sanctuary. There, she poured out her heart to God, with such anguish that Eli the priest thought she was drunk. When she explained that she was in anguish before the Lord, Eli blessed her and assured her that God would answer her prayer. Hannah had touched the heart of God with her tears.

Hannah became the mother of Samuel, the last judge and a great prophet of Israel who anointed the first two kings of Israel, Saul and David.

119

From the Scriptures:

[Elkanah] had two wives; the name of the one was Hannah, and the name of the other Peninnah: and Peninnah had children, but Hannah had no children.

And this man went up out of his city yearly to worship and to sacrifice unto the LORD of hosts in Shiloh. . . .

And when the time was that Elkanah offered, he gave to Peninnah his wife, and to all her sons and her daughters, portions:

But unto Hannah he gave a worthy portion; for he loved Hannah: but the LORD had shut up her womb.

And her adversary also provoked her sore, for to make her fret, because the LORD had shut up her womb.

And as he did so year by year, when she went up to the house of the LORD, so she provoked her; therefore she wept, and did not eat.

Then said Elkanah her husband to her, Hannah, why weepest thou? and why eatest thou not? and why is thy heart grieved? am not I better to thee than ten sons?

So Hannah rose up after they had eaten in Shiloh, and after they had drunk. Now Eli the priest sat upon a seat by a post of the temple of the LORD.

And she was in bitterness of soul, and prayed unto the LORD, and wept sore.

And she vowed a vow, and said, O LORD of hosts, if thou wilt indeed look on the affliction of thine hand-maid, and remember me, and not forget thine hand-maid, but wilt give unto thine handmaid a man child, then I will give him unto the LORD all the days of his life, and there shall no razor come upon his head.

And it came to pass, as she continued praying before the LORD, that Eli marked her mouth.

Now Hannah, she spake in her heart; only her lips moved, but her voice was not heard: therefore Eli thought she had been drunken.

And Eli said unto her, How long wilt thou be drunken? put away thy wine from thee.

And Hannah answered and said, No, my lord, I am a woman of a sorrowful spirit: I have drunk nei-ther wine nor strong drink, but have poured out my soul before the LORD.

Count not thine handmaid for a daughter of Belial: for out of the abundance of my complaint and grief have I spoken hitherto.

Then Eli answered and said, Go in peace: and the God of Israel grant thee thy petition that thou hast asked of him.

— 1 Samuel 1:2–17

121

∾ Twenty-One ∾

You Were Made to Express Emotions

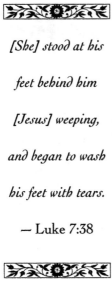

[She] stood at his

feet behind him

[Jesus] weeping,

and began to wash

his feet with tears.

— Luke 7:38

God made men and women very differently. He brought us forth at different stages in His process of creation. The woman was at the peak of God's creative crescendo. God outdid Himself when He brought her forth.

God waited until everything was in place before He brought forth woman. When He made Adam, Adam had everything in creation under his dominion, but he did not have a helpmate.

123

Adam had existed without a relationship, although he did have authority. Men today often find that they can exist without a relationship with a woman. They tend not to be as relationship oriented as women. They direct their energy instead into their work, their career, in which they have power and authority. Positions and titles are important to men, often far more so than relationships.

When women get together, they talk about relationships. They don't even have to know each other very well before they are willing to whip out baby pictures of all their children and grandchildren. Those children might be forty years old now, but they still carry their baby pictures! Women are happy to tell all the details about their family members — how old they are, where they go to school, what they are doing in their lives, whether they are married or not. You won't see an average man whipping out his wallet to show another man his grandbabies.

This doesn't mean that men don't love their children and grandchildren. They just have a different way of expressing that love. They don't spend the majority of their time talking about relationships. Women do, however.

Because women are so relationship oriented, they have a sensitivity toward worship — about nurturing their relationship with God — that men don't have. They have a degree of understanding about spiritual matters that most men don't have. Women seem to understand readily what it means to enter into praise and to long for intimate relationship with God, but men have to be wooed into that desire.

Now what does this have to do with your emotions?

Women are more emotional than men because emotions are the language of relationship. In fact, the more relationship oriented you are, the more emotional you are likely to be.

There's nothing wrong with our being emotional. It's a part of our creation to express our emotions. Emotions are a key part of the way we relate to one another and to God. What's wrong is when we allow ourselves to be led by our emotions — when we allow our emotions to be more important or to carry more weight than our spirits.

Men are often conditioned not to express their emotions. They are taught from an early age to stifle and suppress their emotions. I've seen mothers tell their eighteen-month-old sons, "Stop crying and be a man!" When that boy grows to be a fifty-year-old man, he's likely to have trouble hugging his wife or raising his hands in praise.

When God saw that it was not good for Adam to be alone, He put Adam to sleep and said, "Adam, everything you need has already been put within you. I'm going to pull what you are thirsting for out of you." When Adam opened his eyes, he saw Eve and instantly he was attracted to her.

Adam wasn't attracted to Eve because of her beauty — her figure, face, or her form. He said, "She is me. She is bone of my bone and flesh of my flesh. She is me, only with a womb. She is me with the ability to carry life. She is the feminine expression of my masculinity. She is my release. She is the silk, the rose, the lace, the fragrance, the softness of my life." Adam found in Eve all of the emotions he had longed to express but hadn't been able to release.

Women, don't let anyone convince you that you need to stifle your emotions.

Don't let anything happen to you that makes you so cold you lose your ability to love.

125

Don't rehearse old memories until you become imprisoned by them to the point where you can no longer cry or shout or laugh.

You have a great capacity as a woman to express feelings and affections. God gave you that capacity so you could relate more fully to other people and to Him.

Some women today are in shock. They've lost their sensitivity, their femininity, their ability to feel. When that happens, they've adopted a male stance. They've lost part of their identity, the part that makes them uniquely woman. In fact, when a woman begins to display masculine tendencies, I consider that something has put her femininity into shock.

A person who has been in shock sometimes appears as if she has passed out. She withdraws. She loses touch with the reality around her.

She needs to be warmed and helped and comforted. She needs to be encouraged . . .

Come out of it.

Come out of it!

COME OUT OF IT!

Some women go into shock because they have been mistreated.

Some women go into shock because they have been abused.

Some women go into shock because they have been hurt or rejected.

The time is now for them to come out of it! If you are such a woman, hear me clearly: The time has come for you to come out of your shock! Allow yourself to feel again.

126

Allow yourself to cry again. Allow yourself to cry out to God again.

A person in shock is immobilized. She has let a part of her become paralyzed. She has let her emotions die.

Don't let that happen to you.

If it's already happened, then don't stay in that condition! It's time for you to come out of the state of shock that you are in.

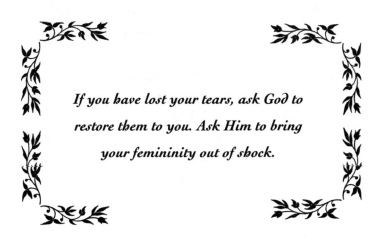

If you have lost your tears, ask God to restore them to you. Ask Him to bring your femininity out of shock.

127

~ *Twenty-Two* ~

Your Emotions and Your Spirit

And the very God of peace sanctify you wholly; and I pray God your whole spirit and soul and body be preserved blameless unto the coming of our Lord Jesus Christ.

— 1 Thessalonians 5:23

We must understand the difference between our spirits and our emotions. They are linked, yet they are separate. Our emotions are part of our soul realm.

In our spirits, we have God-consciousness. Jesus said, "But the hour cometh, and now is, when the true worshipers shall worship the Father in spirit and in truth: for the Father seeketh such to worship him. God is a Spirit: and they that worship him must worship him in spirit and in truth" (John 4:23–24). Paul wrote, "The Spirit itself beareth witness with our spirit, that we are the children of God" (Romans 8:16).

The spirit realm is the realm in which we relate to God intimately and fully.

In our bodies, we have world-consciousness, an awareness of our physical world. If we didn't have bodies, we wouldn't know whether it was a cold day or a hot day. Our bodies are our means of relating to everything in the natural realm.

In our souls, we have self-consciousness. We know that we exist. When God made man, man became a living soul. He became aware of himself.

Now, we each know who we are. It is our self-consciousness, our self-awareness that separates us from oak trees and rushing streams and mountain peaks. It is in our soul realm that we become aware of our emotions and our appetites and our dreams and our memories and our affections. We know we are alive because we have a soul. It is from our soul that we relate to one another as human beings.

How we each express our soulish lives is just as unique as our fingerprints. Even if we were all gathered in one room and shouted "Hallelujah" at the same time, we each would mean something different with our shout of praise. We would have different reasons for voicing our praise. We would have a different understanding of the object of our praise. Only God is capable of hearing the same word from the mouths of a thousand people and understanding fully the thousand meanings that are being expressed.

Truth seems to come to the body of Christ in waves. The Bible says that the "earth shall be full of the knowledge of the LORD, as the waters cover the sea" (Isaiah 11:9). The waters cover the seas with currents and waves.

We see one aspect of God's truth come into the church as a wave, and then another aspect of God's truth comes in as another wave. At times, it seems as if opinions in the church swing like a pendulum. We need to wait until there is a balance before we come to a conclusion about certain teachings. We need to watch the overall pattern of the waves to see how the tide is falling or rising.

The church went through a time in which there was a great emphasis on what the Greek or Hebrew words mean in the Scriptures. It was an intellectual wave that allowed for very little emotional expression of praise and worship. People could explain what the Bible meant, but they didn't know how to do what the Bible talked about when it came to miracles and to the various gifts of the Spirit. During that wave, if a person broke out into praise and worship, their behavior would be denounced as "too emotional." The church didn't know how to handle emotions. We are still learning a lot about how to express our emotions in the church.

130

To tell a person not to be emotional is to tell a person not to be human. It is to deny that person's God-given right and privilege to enter into adoration of the Creator. It is to deny the soul realm. Don't ever try to tell me that God doesn't care about how I feel. I know that He does.

That is one of the reasons I'm in the church. I'm tired of being around people in the world who don't care how I feel — or how anybody else feels for that matter. I want to be in a place where at least some of the people care about how I feel, and where I know I can be with God who always cares about how I feel.

Because of the uniqueness of woman's femininity and her ability to express emotions, there were times in history that God specifically called for women. For example, Jeremiah said, "Call for the mourning women, that they may come" (Jeremiah 9:17). God wanted to see tears and brokenness on the altar. He wanted to hear expressions of sorrow over the fact that His people were being carried away in bondage. He said, "Get the women and tell them to cry."

If ever we needed women to lay on the altar and wail in response to God's people being taken into bondage, it is now!

God knows the power of tears, of feelings. Jesus said about prayer, "What things soever ye desire, when ye pray, believe that ye receive them, and ye shall have them" (Mark 11:24). When you desire something, you don't just "want" it. To desire something is to want it with passion. Jesus said, "Make known to Me the things that you can't do without, the things that you want with a passion."

Man looks on the outer appearance but God looks on the heart. He is looking to see what we desire with all of our heart, not what we want as a whim or an idea in our minds.

131

Is there something today that you want so much that you are willing to lay on the altar and cry for it?

Is there a desire in you to see God move in your life — a desire that is burning in your innermost being with such a passion that you can't forget it, can't get away from it, can't dismiss it, and can't ignore it?

Is there something that you want to see God do with such intensity that you awaken in the middle of the night with the thought of it?

Is there something that you feel so certain that God wants to do and will do that you just know that it is going

to be done, even if every indicator around you says otherwise?

That is your desire. It arises from your spirit and it's
meant to be expressed by your soul. It is something God
expects you to be emotional about!

*What is it that you want God to
do for you today? Do you want
it with all of your heart? Do you
want it with passion and intensity?*

Twenty-Three

Touching God With Your Feelings

Seeing then that we have a great high priest, that is passed into the heavens, Jesus the Son of God, let us hold fast our profession. For we have not an high priest which cannot be touched with the feeling of our infirmities; but was in all points tempted like as we are, yet without sin. Let us therefore come boldly unto the throne of grace, that we may obtain mercy, and find grace to help in time of need.

— Hebrews 4:14–16

Some things are things that only God can do. Hannah knew that.

From the world's standpoint, Hannah had a good life. She had a good husband. He was a rich man. He was a good man. He was generous to her. He loved her greatly. He said to her, "Am not I better to you than ten sons?" But he hadn't given her a son.

Hannah didn't have the one thing she truly desired — a son who could worship God as a priest. And she knew that only God could give her the desire of her heart. She went to the right place with her prayer request.

There are many things that God expects us to do, but

133

there are some things that only God can do. And God expects us to call upon Him to do those things that are His "job."

Is there a need in your life that is a job for God? Have you taken that problem to Him? Or have you taken it to everybody else and sought out every other solution but God? If so, it's time to stop playing games and get serious with God.

Stop running to this group or that group. Stop trying to use this method or that method. Go to God. There are jobs that only God can do. Going to anybody else and trying any other method is a waste of your time.

Don't even think about going to the palm reader . . .

the dope man . . .

the crack house . . .

or the loan shark. Go to the altar and cry out to God! Express yourself with intensity.

134

God gave you feelings so you could light the altar of incense — so that you might "burn" about something to the point that when you put your believing to your feeling, it's as if you have put a match to incense. Your prayer then floats up to God like a sweet-smelling savor!

No two blends of incense smell the same. And the same is true for your prayer. The way you pray and the words you use and the intent of your heart are all about you. Don't pray the prayer of someone else. Don't say to yourself, "Well, that prayer worked for her. Perhaps it will work for me." God is looking for a prayer that comes up out of your passion, your desire, your emotions, your soul!

You may have read all the recipes for prayer that have ever been written. There are a lot of them around. Five steps for a miracle. Three steps to a blessing. Four steps for binding the devil over your house. Four steps to come into financial prosperity. Two ways to evoke the power and the love of God.

Before we had all those recipes, however, we had women who were willing to cry upon the altar of the Lord and say nothing more than, "Do this for me, Jesus! If You don't, I will die!" They didn't have a process or a formula. Just the power of their passion. And God heard their prayers and answered them.

Do you really want to see God move?

Really?

Really?

Really?

Then touch God with your passion. . . touch Him with your feelings . . .

with your getting up in the middle of the night and pacing the floor . . .

with your tears that flow like a flood from your eyes . . .

with your groanings and wailings.

We have a High Priest, Jesus Christ, who is not touched by your outer holiness, your degree, your BMW, your fur coat, your diamond ring, or by how cute you are. He is a High Priest who is only touched by your boldness to come before His throne of grace and cry out with your faith for what it is that you need from Him.

135

He is not swayed by the fact of your need. You may be broke, busted, and disgusted, but those conditions don't sway Him. He is moved by the depth of your desire that is matched by the depth of your faith! He is touched by your feeling and your believing.

You may say, "I can't touch God. I messed up and I had a baby out of wedlock and I've been divorced three times." God isn't touched by how good you've been or by how bad you've been. He is touched by the feeling of your infirmities. He is moved by your cry that comes up out of your weakness.

If there is any ember still glowing in your heart, any flicker of faith still burning in your spirit, fan that ember, fan that flicker into a flame of desire and call out to God.

Can you still feel?

Then God can still be moved on your behalf.

You may be weak.

136

You may have failed.

You may have sinned.

But if you still have feeling toward God and you still have a desire in your heart to see God move on your behalf . . .

Then God can still be moved.

You may not have what someone else has.

You may not look like that other person looks.

You may not have that woman's talents or another woman's skills.

You may not have her education or her personality or her background.

But none of that matters.

None of that moves God.

He is moved by the feelings of your infirmities.

God is not moved by what you have.

He is moved by how you feel about what you don't have and what you need. He is moved by what you are believing for with your faith.

Go to God today with your need and express your need to Him with the full force of your feelings and faith.

❧ *Twenty-Four* ❧

What Do You Want Enough to Cry for It?

Hannah answered

and said . . .

I am a woman of a

sorrowful spirit:

I have drunk neither

wine nor strong

drink, but have

poured out my soul

before the LORD.

— 1 Samuel 1:15

Hannah was a woman who wanted something so much that she was willing to cry for it.

She slipped into the temple one night and folded up her face like a towel and wrenched her tear ducts like a garment and wept until the high priest Eli thought she was drunk. She said, "No, I haven't been drinking. I am a wounded woman with a sorrowful spirit!"

Are you so filled with the idea that your life might be different that you are willing to stagger to the altar and pray while others play?

Do you want something from God with so much desire that you are willing to risk the opinions of others who might say that you are too emotional in your asking God to give it to you?

138

Do you believe with such a passion that you are intoxicated with the hope of what God has for you?

What hope or dream do you have that consumes your thinking, your feeling, your believing? Pray about that . . . because if your prayer request doesn't move you, it probably won't move God.

Use your trouble, too, to fuel your passion.

The very fear that has been tormenting you . . .
the very problem that has been traumatizing you . . .
is the very thing that is going to enable you to touch God.

How can that be?

The depth of the trouble you have been experiencing is likely to be equal to the depth of the desire that drives you toward God.

The greater your problem . . .

The more intense your fear . . .

The deeper your discouragement . . .

The more you are willing to risk crying out to God. When your trouble is great enough and your desire is strong enough, you will feel that you have nothing to lose, and everything to gain by pouring out all your passion to God.

There are women who need to stop worrying so much about being Miss Wonderful that they stifle their emotions before God. There are women who need to stop weighing everything they do with the idea that they need to uphold their reputation so they can belong to the right club and get in with the right group and have the favor of the right crowd.

139

God wants women who will humble themselves before Him, who will come to Him, who will cry out to Him — without any thought to what other people think or say.

Make a decision that you are going to allow yourself to touch God with intensity. Don't hold anything back. Cry for what you want as if your very life depends upon it.

Rachel said to Jacob, "Give me a child, lest I die." She wanted something so much that if she couldn't have it and live, she would rather die. Go to God with that same attitude.

God is looking for women who want to see God's will done on this earth so much that they will cry for it. He is looking for women who want to see right become victorious over wrong, good win over evil, Jesus reign over the devil. He is looking for women who want to see God act on their behalf — and who want it so much they will cry aloud for it and will refuse to be silenced. He wants women who will cry and not shut up!

The power of life and death is in your tongue. Refuse to be silenced. Speak life! After you have prayed, speak God's words of life to yourself. Speak them to your problem. Speak them to your circumstance . . .

your situation . . .

your need . . .

your problem . . .

your lack of supply.

Don't allow yourself to be intimidated into remaining quiet about what it is that you want God to do for you. Cry for it!

God will hear and answer

the cry of your heart.

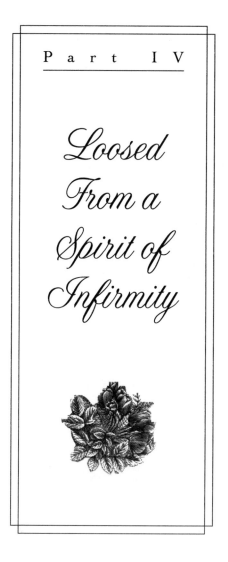

Part I V

*Loosed
From a
Spirit of
Infirmity*

❧ An Infirm Woman ❧

While teaching in a synagogue, Jesus encountered a woman who had been "bent over" or "doubled up" for eighteen years. She was bound by a spirit of infirmity. When Jesus saw her, He was moved with compassion toward her and called to her, "Woman, thou art loosed." He laid His hands upon her and immediately she could stand up straight. Her response was to glorify God in spite of the criticism that followed for Jesus having worked this deliverance miracle on the Sabbath.

From the Scriptures:

And he [Jesus] was teaching in one of the synagogues on the sabbath.

And, behold, there was a woman which had a spirit of infirmity eighteen years, and was bowed together, and could in no wise lift up herself.

And when Jesus saw her, he called her to him, and said unto her, Woman, thou art loosed from thine infirmity.

And he laid his hands on her: and immediately she was made straight, and glorified God.

And the ruler of the synagogue answered with indignation, because that Jesus had healed on the sabbath day, and said unto the people, There are six days in which men ought to work: in them therefore come and be healed, and not on the sabbath day.

The Lord then answered him, and said, Thou hypocrite, doth not each one of you on the sabbath loose his ox or his ass from the stall, and lead him away to watering?

145
∾

And ought not this woman, being a daughter of Abraham, whom Satan hath bound, lo, these eighteen years, be loosed from this bond on the sabbath day?

— Luke 13:10–16

146

~ *Twenty-Five* ~

The Nature
of Your Deliverance

Help us, O God of

our salvation, for

the glory of thy

name: and deliver

us . . . for thy

name's sake.

— Psalm 79:9

The woman whom Jesus encountered on the Sabbath was a woman who came to the synagogue with a spirit of infirmity, and who left the synagogue that day loosed from it.

Now I want you to notice that the Bible does not say that Jesus destroyed the infirmity itself so that it could never exist again in her life or the life of another person. Rather, He simply separated this infirmity from this woman. He removed any influence of the infirmity from her life.

147

I know many people today who are waiting for the thing that has restricted or inhibited them to be destroyed. They don't think they can be loosed, or feel free unless the source of their infirmity dies. They must awaken to the possibility that a source of infirmity can continue to exist, and yet have no influence or impact upon them.

The Bible says that Jesus was manifested to "destroy the works of the devil." (See 1 John 3:8.) That word *destroy* in the Greek language means to dismantle, decompose, or break down. Whatever Satan has built up, Jesus breaks down. Something may exist, but be powerless to work against you. It's still there, but it doesn't work. It ceases to be effective.

Hell becomes very confused when Jesus delivers a person from a spirit of infirmity. Satan has a file that is supposed to predict precisely what is going to work on you. If it doesn't work, there's confusion.

Satan starts grilling his demons . . .

Didn't you catch her at a weak moment?

Didn't you make the temptation enticing enough?

Didn't you make the accusation strong enough?

Didn't you bind that spirit of infirmity to her with strong enough chains?

148

And the demons reply "yes" to all the questions and then add, "But this time it just didn't work."

It isn't that Satan doesn't try to bind a person who has been set free. But rather, that what had worked on you in the past no longer works. You have been loosed from its effectiveness.

In Mark 2:1–12 we read about a man who had palsy. Four of his friends brought him to Jesus and lowered him through the ceiling so Jesus could heal him. Jesus said to him, "Arise, and take up thy bed, and go thy way into thine house" (Mark 2:11). This man was carried to Jesus while he was lying on his bed. He left Jesus carrying his bed on his back. The two — the man and the bed — traded places!

We are never going to be entirely free of all problems. And, there are some specific problems from which we may not be entirely freed. But Jesus comes to heal us and deliver us so that the problem ceases to control us, diminish us, hold us back, or keep us down. Instead of the problem controlling us, we have control over the problem in the name of Jesus.

I believe that many people have been taught incorrectly about deliverance. As a result, they expect something that is unrealistic. They expect to walk down a prayer line and have somebody lay hands on them with such power that the devil will never be able to say another word to them for the rest of their lives. They think if they get in the right church or sit under the right ministry, they will become so mature in Christ that they will never be tempted again — they'll be completely "delivered" from any possibility of the devil ever getting their attention or speaking to them. It'll never happen. That isn't what deliverance means.

Deliverance means that the thing that used to control you is now under your control. Deliverance means that the thing that sat on the throne of your heart and ruled with power over your life has been dethroned and replaced by Jesus Christ. It still exists, but it isn't in charge.

Every now and then, Satan will attempt a coup. He'll try to regain control over the throne of your life. And at that point it is up to you to resist his effort and trust in God and exert control with your will. Satan isn't going to stop trying. Deliverance, however, puts you in position to keep him from succeeding.

149

For example, God isn't going to remove your temper from you. If you have struggled with angry outbursts and have desired to be delivered from your own temper, God will give you power over your tongue and control over your temper. But He isn't going to remove your temper from you. You need to have a temper or you would never feel compelled to rise up and do spiritual battle against evil. There's some evil in this world that you need to get "hot" about so you will pray against it and stand against it and battle against it in the spirit realm.

We find the word *wrath* linked to God in a number of places in the Bible. That word means "angry with fire." God gets angry with fire when He is challenged by evil or when He sees evil destroying His innocent children. It's good for you to get upset over evil when it comes at you.

What God will do in delivering you from your own temper is to impart to you the Holy Spirit's anointing in your life so you can deal with your temper and control it.

I once had a woman come to me and say, "Bishop, I have a problem with the flesh." Now there are many things that are rightfully associated with the flesh but when a person says that she has "problems with the flesh" we always tend to think of one thing, right? We think of sexual lust. She said, "Bishop, I want to be delivered from this flesh problem. I want you to pray that the Lord will just take it away!"

I said to her, "Are you sure that is what you want? Are you sure you don't ever want to feel any sexual feelings or sexual desires again?"

When I explained it like that, she had second thoughts! She didn't want to lose her sexuality; she just wanted to have control over her sexual desires and appetites. She wanted God to impart to her the power to say "no" to her own lust.

What we want is not to be a slave to our own passions, our own emotions, our own desires, our own appetites, but to enjoy them and let them serve to glorify God. That is the true nature of deliverance in the vast majority of cases.

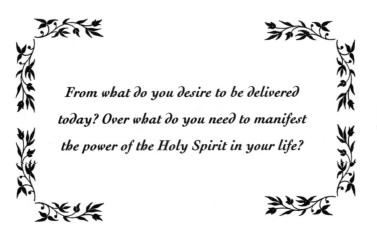

From what do you desire to be delivered today? Over what do you need to manifest the power of the Holy Spirit in your life?

151

∽ *Twenty-Six* ∾

An Inner Work

He halted upon

his thigh . . .

because he touched

the hollow of Jacob's

thigh.

— Genesis 32:31,32

Jacob wrestled with an angel of the Lord one night and came out of that experience with two things: the blessing of God and a limp in his walk. He limped all the rest of his life.

The limp didn't mean Jacob hadn't been blessed by God. It meant only that he had a limp.

Your struggle with sin doesn't mean that you aren't saved in your spirit or healed in your soul. It means only that you still have a limp.

And the fact is, you may never lose your limp entirely. Most of us won't.

We may learn to walk, and even to skip and run with our limp. We may learn to get around so well that nothing about our limp slows us down.

We may be able to get a built-up shoe that disguises our limp and enables us to function as near to normal as possible.

We may forget that our limp is there — it may come to mean absolutely nothing to us.

When that happens, and we feel no pain and no self-consciousness about our limp, then we are healed, even though the limp may remain.

My children recently saw a man who had lost the use of his legs. They said, "Why don't you come to have our daddy pray for you."

The man said, "Oh, I'm alright now. I am healed."

They didn't understand what he meant so he explained, "You see, when this first happened, I was in pain all of the time. I know I'm healed because it doesn't hurt any more."

Don't let the limp fool you. You can be healed and still have a limp. The limp is only a sign that you have been through something, not that you are still struggling with something or in pain over something.

If you can think about something and it doesn't hurt any more, you have been healed.

If you can talk about a painful experience in your past and it doesn't cause you to feel anger or hatred, you have been healed.

153

If you can see that person who wronged or hurt you and you don't feel bitterness, you have been healed.

You may still have scars on your body. You may still be divorced. You may still have a need. You may still have the "limp," but on the inside you have been healed.

Don't confuse the outer symptoms with the inner work. The symptoms are not what define you. What God has done in your innermost being is what defines you.

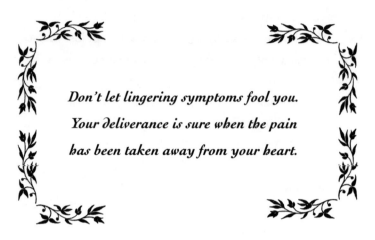

Don't let lingering symptoms fool you.
Your deliverance is sure when the pain
has been taken away from your heart.

154

Twenty-Seven

Loosed From Whom?

Lead us not into temptation, but deliver us from evil.

— Matthew 6:13

Long after I was saved, I still thought I needed to be delivered from the devil. The popular phrase at the time was, "The devil made me do it." Well, I didn't want the devil to make me do anything so I prayed hard to be delivered from the devil.

After a while I realized that the devil wasn't the problem. I stopped wasting my time and breath praying about the devil. I changed my prayer, "Lord, save me from me. Please don't let me kill my crazy self. Please don't let me do myself in — physically, emotionally, mentally, or any other way. Deliver me from my own evil tendencies."

Sometimes people don't blame the devil, but rather, they blame other people or a specific person or group of people. The greater fact is this: It isn't what people say about you or to you that's going to matter in the long run. It's what you say about yourself to yourself.

A spirit of infirmity is not a bondage that another person places on your life. It's not a bondage of chains and shackles and prison bars on the outside of you. It's a bondage on the inside. And you can't walk away from a

155

bondage that is on the inside of you. It will keep you locked up . . . until you quit agreeing with the person who has mistreated you.

My wife and I counseled a woman that literally couldn't leave the house even though her wife-beating husband was gone. She'd get as far as the door and have an attack in which she could hardly breathe. His presence and his blows weren't the main reason she was in bondage. She was in bondage primarily because of the way she felt about herself. She had allowed his blows to beat down her self-esteem until there was virtually no self and no esteem left.

Jesus asked His disciples, "Who do men say that I am?" They gave Him all the latest gossip: Some say You are John, some say Elijah, some say Jeremiah, some say one of the other prophets. Jesus said, "I'm not concerned about what some say. Who do you say that I am?" (See Matthew 16:13–15.)

"Some say" won't hurt anybody.

"You say" will. It can make all the difference in your life.

So many people I know have made it their life's work to change somebody's opinion about them. They are determined to prove that they are worthy or valuable in that other person's eyes. Their goal in life is to show somebody that they are good, that they are a Christian, that they are important.

Never allow another person's good opinion of you to be your goal. The fact is, they might never like you. They may never approve of you, consider you to be important, or call you good. They may never change their opinion of you.

If you agree with the person who rejects you or abuses you, then you put yourself into bondage. If you say, "Yes, they were right to hit me — I'm worthy to be hit. Yes, they were right to leave me — I'm worthy to be left. Yes, they were right to hurt me — I'm worthy to be hurt" . . . then you are tying yourself up with their opinion rather than tying yourself into God's opinion of you. When their bad opinion of you becomes your bad opinion of you, there's a prison built inside your soul with only one prisoner in it — you.

Are you prepared to deal with the fact that the person you've spent your entire life trying to impress may never be impressed? Are you prepared to face the reality that from God's perspective, it doesn't matter one way or the other if he or she is impressed or not impressed?

I encourage you to come to the conclusion I reached a long time ago: People are crazy.

157

That's not a great theological truth but it's good practical common sense. You will never be able to figure out why some people do what they do. You'll never be able to predict all the foibles and quirks and eccentricities of human nature. You'll find yourself shaking your head all the way through life saying, "Why did she do that? Why did he allow that?" The only explanation is that people are crazy.

That's why God called you to worship Himself, not people. You won't get anywhere by worshiping a person, which is what you are doing if you are seeking that person's approval as the most defining opinion about your life.

You see, the wonderful thing about God is that He doesn't meet with the board or a committee before He decides to bless you. He doesn't have to get anybody else's approval before He pours out His love to you. He doesn't consult anybody about you!

Don't get me wrong — I like people. I just know what to expect and what not to expect from them. If you're not careful, the craziness of other people will drive you crazy. If you are going to deal effectively with people in this world, you have got to be able to work right alongside them but not allow yourself to be controlled or governed by their opinion of you.

The deliverance you likely need most is not a deliverance from the devil or a deliverance from another person. The deliverance you probably need most is a deliverance from something in your own heart and mind.

158

Ask the Lord today to open the prison doors of your own soul and set you free.

∽ Twenty-Eight ∾
Your Tailor-Made Infirmity

Woman, thou art

loosed from thine

infirmity.

— Luke 13:12

Every woman has her own tailor-made infirmity. The enemy has been studying you all your life, checking you out, figuring out which temptation will work best on you. He's not going to bring you ice cream if you like chocolate. He knows your weaknesses and what is most likely to tempt you to sin.

In case you haven't experienced this truth yet, let me tell you that church people are very prejudiced when it comes to sin. They tend to classify sin into two categories: acceptable and unacceptable. The particular sin you have will fall into the acceptable category if a person can relate to your sin — in other words, if he or she has that sin in their life, too. It will fall into the unacceptable category if it's not their particular weakness or experience.

They will forgive you quickly if it's something they can relate to, but if it's something they can't relate to, they will condemn you to hell without a judge, jury, or trial.

I once had an experience with another minister who I considered to be very arrogant and proud. Now, my father was from Mississippi and my mother was from Alabama so I have always considered myself to be a cornbread, collard-green, down-home kind of guy. I consider myself an ordinary person. I don't need a lot of pomp and circumstance in my life. There's no report to be written on me. I'm just a guy who God uses and when it comes right down to it, I'm just a lump of clay in motion. I like to be "normal." I don't want to be put up on any pedestal.

This other man likes walking into a room and having everybody fall prostrate while they are singing "All Hail to Jesus." I'm exaggerating, of course — but not by much. He speaks in a deep resonating voice aimed at impressing anybody who hears him. People with super-inflated egos like that are a problem to me. You might even say my irritation with them is my infirmity. I want to get a little blow dart and aim it at them and pop their balloon and watch them fly into a fizzle all over the room.

Now this man didn't like me any more than I liked him. We were too civil to confront each other about our mutual dislike, but if I saw him coming, I'd veer left, and if he saw me coming, he'd veer right. We did our best to ignore each other. If we were forced to come face to face, we'd say, "Hi, brother! How are you? Praise the Lord!" and we'd go on our respective ways as quickly as possible.

One day the Lord spoke to me and said, "Do you know that problem you have with the minister you dislike so much?"

"Yes, Lord."

"It's your fault."

I nearly came unglued. "What? My fault? Do you know how arrogant and proud he is?"

I spent a considerable time telling the Lord how right I was and how wrong he was and how justified I was to hold my opinion. When I was done the Lord said, "Aren't you something? If that brother had a weakness in an area where you have a weakness, you'd have all the patience in the world with him. But the moment I send somebody into your life who has a weakness in an area where you are strong, you have the nerve to be judgmental."

I almost died. I could hardly breathe. I said, "Lord, I don't mind You doing surgery, but this time you punched a knife into my chest without an anesthetic."

God was right, of course. He always is.

We all tend to gravitate toward people who have our own infirmities. And there's a danger in that. If we hang around people who have our set of infirmities, we become codependent on them. We feed the sin in them and they feed the sin in us. We allow their weakness to continue and they allow our weakness to continue. Instead of healing one another, we make one another worse. It is God's mercy and God's plan to bring people into our lives who are strong in areas where we are weak, and people who are weak in areas where we are

161

strong. That way we can help one another and bring balance to the body of Christ.

One of your greatest tests in life will be to live in a covenant relationship of God's love with a person who has a weakness that you don't have and to which you can't relate.

When Satan sends his demons out to oppress you, they already have a portfolio on you. They know just the right buttons to push in you. They know your particular infirmities.

Those demons know if your father never liked you . . . and if your mother approved of your older sister but not you . . .

and if your boyfriend rejected you and started going with your best friend . . .

and if a teacher held you up for ridicule. They have an entire profile worked up on you so that they won't have to waste time experimenting on which temptations are going to work best. They know where you are vulnerable.

Jesus said to the woman with a spirit of infirmity, "Woman, thou art loosed from thine infirmity." Jesus knew her exact infirmity. He knew the very thing that had her bound up and bent over.

He knows about your infirmity, too. His word to you today is, "I'm going to loose you."

Get ready for Him to do it.

162

Have you identified your infirmity?
Are you ready for God to deliver
you from it?

163

∽ Twenty-Nine ∽

Lose What You've Been Loosed From!

Go,

and sin

no more.

— John 8:11

When this woman was loosed from her infirmity, she was made straight immediately.

Don't make the error of thinking that your deliverance must take a long time. Change can happen in an instant. You can arrive immediately at an understanding of the truth. It's as if a light comes on.

164

In fact, I think the best form of change is sudden change. Years ago I smoked and I tried to quit smoking by cutting down to fifteen cigarettes a day and then ten and so forth. That was slow torture. One day I just threw the pack away and said, "I'm done with it." That was the end of cigarette smoking for me. The change was made!

Change means you were and now you aren't. Period.

You can be in an ungodly affair and leave that affair whether your partner in it agrees or disagrees, whether he's around or not. When you stop needing what it is that you were needing, the affair is over. When you are loosed from the need that drove you to that affair, you don't need to meet with that person or try to figure things out with that person. When you unhook from them inside yourself, you're free. You can just walk away and say, "I'm done with that. I'm not vulnerable in that way anymore."

There doesn't need to be any long, drawn-out discussion or any major confrontation or any redefining. As far as I'm concerned, you're better off without any of that. Just say, "I'm out of here" and be gone.

Now I'm not talking about husbands and wives. I'm talking about your association with ungodly people who have hurt you, rejected you, abused you, or used you. Once you are delivered, don't hang around. Get moving and get out. Get as far away as you can, as fast as you can.

People who have abused or used you aren't going to take kindly to your wanting to redefine your relationship with them. They've been on a power trip regarding you and they aren't interested in losing power or control. They aren't going to like the fact that you no longer are going to allow them to manipulate you.

Just leave.

Recognize, too, that any time God looses you from something, He has in mind something else to which He wants you to be attached. Things that are completely loosed — things that are totally on their own without any connection — die. They wither and shrivel up. Nothing can exist totally on its own and remain vital and alive.

If you pull a plant up out of the ground, it might look good for a day or two, but then it's going to wither and die. If you isolate a person and put her in an isolation chamber for very long, she'll curl up in a ball and be totally useless. We all need to be connected. It's a matter,

165

however, of being connected to the right things. Connection isn't the issue. Connected to what is the issue.

If God looses you from an infirmity and you aren't reconnected to something good and positive in your life, you are likely to seek out any old reconnection. You might even go back to the thing to which you were originally connected just because it's familiar.

How many times do we see that happen? People are freed from a relationship that has been negative and they end up going right back to it because it's familiar — even though they don't want to return to that relationship, even though they know the person isn't right for them, even though they know God doesn't want that relationship in their life.

Often people will even reconnect with things they hate just for the sake of being reconnected. They don't like it, they don't want it, but they are used to it.

I've seen women go from one abusive relationship to another. They don't like being abused. But the pain of abuse has become familiar to them and they'd rather have the pain of abuse than remain disconnected.

Refuse to reconnect with your infirmity.

When you are loosed, stay loosed.

Don't allow yourself to go back into bondage.

Once you are free, stay free!

Give God Your Praise

She was made

straight, and

glorified God.

— Luke 13:13

When this woman with a spirit of infirmity was loosed and made straight, she immediately glorified God. Nobody else. Only God.

I refuse to glorify anybody but God. I know that all of my needs are met by Him. I know that my identity comes from Him. I know that all my help and all my forgiveness have come from Him.

Therefore, don't try to put a guilt trip on me for not acknowledging all that you think you may have done for me. It won't work. I'm not going to give you any other credit than the fact that God may have used you to bless me. He's my Helper. He's my Deliverer.

Father, I stretch my hands to Thee.

I know You will remember Me.

When others forget and leave me all alone,

I know that Jesus, Jesus, Jesus will hear my

groan.

When you give all the glory and all the thanks and all the praise to God for delivering you, people may not understand what you are doing or just why you are so excited. The main reason is that they don't truly know how you feel. They don't know what it's like to have had your particular infirmity, much less what it was like to have had your particular infirmity year after year after year. This woman had suffered with her infirmity for eighteen years. She had been crippled and bent over for so long she didn't know what it was like to look up. Once she was made straight, she couldn't help but give God the glory!

That will be true for you when you are loosed from your infirmity. Other people may not understand. They don't know how you felt then, so they can't understand how you feel now that you're delivered. That's alright.

The way you praise God is the way you praise God. You may want to yell. . .

or cry . . .

or sing . . .

or shout . . .

or dance!

You may want to praise Him with musical instruments. You may want to fall on your face or run like the wind. Praise Him the way you want to praise Him. Don't worry about what other people think of your praise. Get out your praise and give God the glory!

Let me assure you that when drug addicts and homosexuals and adulterers are delivered, they get happy. They can shout praise louder than any other people I know. They know from what they've been delivered!

They know it is God who delivered them! They aren't the least bit bashful about giving God their praise.

Your praise is likely to be related directly to your former pain. The greater the pain, the greater your praise. If you have never been bound, you have no idea how good it feels to be free.

Don't criticize another person for being too emotional in praise. You haven't walked in their shoes. So you can't understand why they are now dancing in their shoes.

If you are in a church that won't let you praise God openly, get into a church that will let you praise Him. God is worthy of our praise. He commands us to praise Him. He dwells in the praises of His people. He delights in your praise.

169

Praise God loud and long today
for all that He has done for you!

∽ *Thirty-One* ∽

Don't Break Your Rhythm

I will bless the

LORD at all times:

his praise shall

continually be

in my mouth.

— Psalm 34:1

Don't break your rhythm of praise for anybody.

No matter what you hear said about you . . .

No matter how people may look at you . . .

No matter what happens . . .

Keep your praise going!

This woman's deliverance caused the ruler of the synagogue to feel indignation. He spoke out against her miracle.

People may not like your deliverance either.

But . . .

It doesn't matter if some people don't speak to you any more . . .

or if some people don't come to visit you anymore . . .

or if some people don't seem to understand you . . .

or if some people don't call you.

You have been loosed by God and therefore, you have a right granted to you by God to stand straight and praise!

Are you aware that you have a God-given privilege to praise God as much as you want? And furthermore, you can be as emotional as you want to be in your praise? Find a place where you can praise God the way you want to praise Him!

People fall all over themselves with excitement about having won a prize on a TV game show, a prize they are going to have to pay taxes on and which they probably can't even use . . . and the world thinks that's okay.

People jump up and down and hug total strangers because their team won the big game in the last few seconds on the game clock — a game that will only be important to them until next week, a game for which they won't even be able to recall the score a month from now . . . and the world says such behavior is normal.

But let people get excited about the way God has delivered them, and let them praise Him with a little emotion — knowing that their lives have been changed for all eternity and that the deepest infirmity of their life no longer has control over them . . . and the world will call them lunatics.

Don't worry about what the world says. For that matter, don't worry about what someone in the church says. You have the privilege and right to praise the God of your deliverance — so praise the Lord!

This woman did the wise thing. She kept her rhythm and let Jesus deal with those who were upset at her

171

deliverance. While she was glorifying God, Jesus dealt with her enemies.

While you are praising God today, the Lord is fighting the battle for you in the heavenlies. He is dealing with the enemy of your soul. He is pulverizing the demonic powers that sought to oppress you and bind you and keep you from God's blessings.

Your praise isn't just an expression of your joy. You actually are doing battle in the spirit realm. While you are praising God, swoop, the angels of God are coming into your hospital room. Swoop, the angels of God are surrounding your child. Swoop, the angels of God are stopping your enemy in his tracks. Swoop, the angels of God are scattering your enemy!

Have you ever praised God — singing and rejoicing — as you drove your car and suddenly, you felt as if you weren't alone? The fact is, you weren't. Swoop, God's angels were there right by your side. You may not see them, but they are there! The Bible says that "the angel of the LORD encampeth round about them that fear him, and delivereth them" (Psalm 34:7).

It's difficult to imagine that someone would get upset that this woman had been healed. It seems that as long as this woman was bent over and needed their help, the people in that synagogue didn't have a problem with her. But as soon as she stood straight and started glorifying God, she became a problem.

And yet, is that any different from what many women experience today?

There are those who like to surround themselves with weak, sick, needy people. But if a woman stands up straight and praises God, they don't quite know what to do with her.

If people are upset with your deliverance and your praise, consider their "upset-ness" to be their problem. Don't try to explain yourself or justify your praise. Don't try to show them how the healed, healthy you is better than the sick you. Just stay standing and keep praising.

There's an undercurrent of criticism that always coexists with praise. There will always be somebody in every praise service who is sitting in the corner criticizing the praise. That critical person may be in your own home — criticizing you as you sing praises to God in the shower. That person may be in your social group — criticizing you for giving thanks and praise to God in the flow of normal conversation. That person may be someone at your place of employment — criticizing you for giving praise to God during a coffee break.

173

Don't pay any attention to them. This woman apparently didn't. She didn't say, "Oh, since you object to what has happened to me, I'll just take on this spirit of infirmity again. I'll just stoop over again in my crippled position for another eighteen years."

Don't give in to the criticism that other people may have about your deliverance. Don't listen to their protests, their murmuring, their gossip, or their attempt to rationalize away your deliverance. Don't let them hurt your feelings or inhibit you.

Sometimes you just have to praise God in the midst of background noise!

Stay standing tall. Keep praising.
Continue to glorify God regardless
of what others may say.

174

∽ *Thirty-Two* ∾

Secure Your Deliverance

> *Stand fast*
>
> *in the faith . . .*
>
> *be strong.*
>
> — 1 Corinthians 16:13

Jesus responded to the man who criticized His deliverance of the woman who had a spirit of infirmity. He said, "Thou hypocrite, doth not each one of you on the sabbath loose his ox or his ass from the stall, and lead him away to watering? And ought not this woman, being a daughter of Abraham, whom Satan hath bound, lo, these eighteen years, be loosed from this bond on the sabbath day?" (Luke 13:15–16)

Oxen were considered very profitable to farmers in those days. They were work animals. The ass was not considered to be as valuable. The ass was often stubborn and contentious, and was useful for very little. Jesus said, "You will loose not only your valuable animal, but your nearly worthless animal on the Sabbath, and yet complain that a human being has been delivered?"

People seem to get very excited when talented folk are delivered. They don't get as excited when ordinary people are set free from their infirmities.

I've got good news for you today — God doesn't make that differentiation. He desires to see needs met for both the highly talented and lesser talented. Your deliverance does not depend upon the scope of your future usefulness or your future ministry. God delivers you because He loves you.

God has delivered countless people who have never written a book about their experience, or who never have gone on to lead the choir or sing a solo or chair a committee or teach a Sunday school class. God's deliverance is not contingent upon what you will do after you are delivered.

This woman of infirmity is never mentioned again. Nevertheless, Jesus delivered her.

I want you to notice also that Jesus reminded them that they kept their ox and ass in stalls. They were not kept close to where the water was flowing freely. If they had been kept close to the flow of water, there would have been no need to loose them on the Sabbath.

Stalls are built by men. They are designed to keep animals closed off and separated. There are stalls today that are man-made. They are used to divide and separate people. They are made to keep people from moving into areas where they can get what they need. People try to keep other people "in their place" so they can control them — so they can lead them to what it is that they want them to have, and to nothing else.

When you are delivered by God, you may need to say "no" to those who have kept you in a stall of their own making.

You may have to say, "I'm free and I'm not going back into that cage."

You may have to say, "I've decided to live close to the living water of the Holy Spirit and I'm not going to be put

176

into a position where I have to rely on you or anybody else to lead me to what it is that you think I need or don't need."

There's a freedom that comes with deliverance that you must secure for yourself. You must refuse to be put back into a stall that keeps you from the things you need, and especially those things that you need on the Sabbath! You must stay close to the water. Stay close to where you can be refreshed.

When God delivers you, He wants you to be delivered from the entire environment in which you were kept cooped up and chained.

If God delivers you from an addiction, He desires to deliver you from the entire environment that contributed to your addiction in the first place. You're going to have to disassociate yourself from the person who dealt drugs to you and used drugs with you and encouraged you to think you needed drugs in the first place. You're going to have to move out of that circle, that environment, maybe even that neighborhood. Get out of the stall! Go where you can be refreshed in the Lord and stay there.

Once you are loosed by Jesus,
refuse to return to the place
where you were in bondage.

177

Part V

Loosed
and Made
Whole

~ A Woman With a Problem ~

A woman who had hemorrhaged for twelve years made her way to Jesus one day. This woman had one of those problems that just wouldn't go away. She had sought help from many physicians, but none of them had been able to help her. As a result, not only was her health worse, but she had spent all of her money.

She faced not only the challenge of forcing her way through the crowd, but the stigma of being considered "unclean" — an outcast, an impure woman. She refused to let either challenge keep her from Jesus. When she touched the hem of His garment, she was healed just as she had believed she would be.

Jesus said to her that her faith had made her whole — not only healed in her body, but fully restored in every area of her life.

181

From the Scriptures:

And a certain woman, which had an issue of blood twelve years,

And had suffered many things of many physicians, and had spent all that she had, and was nothing bettered, but rather grew worse,

When she had heard of Jesus, came in the press behind, and touched his garment.

For she said, If I may touch but his clothes, I shall be whole.

And straightway the fountain of her blood was dried up; and she felt in her body that she was healed of that plague.

And Jesus, immediately knowing in himself that virtue had gone out of him, turned him about in the press, and said, Who touched my clothes?

And his disciples said unto him, Thou seest the multitude thronging thee, and sayest thou, Who touched me?

And he looked round about to see her that had done this thing.

But the woman fearing and trembling, knowing what was done in her, came and fell down before him, and told him all the truth.

And he said unto her, Daughter, thy faith hath made thee whole; go in peace, and be whole of thy plague.

— Mark 5:25–34

Thirty-Three

The Drain
on Your Life

And a certain

woman, which had

an issue of blood

twelve years.

— Mark 5:25

I don't know her name. I don't know who her father was or who her husband was. I don't know where she lived or how she lived. I don't know if she was rich or poor.

She could have been any woman. She may have been every woman. The Bible refers to her only as a woman with an "issue of blood." The Lord may have referred to her in such a generic manner so that any woman could relate to her and put their name in her place.

To have an issue of blood is normal for a woman. This woman's problem was that her issue of blood had lasted too long. She is a woman who had a problem that lingered. It didn't go away. It stayed around, and then stayed on and stayed on.

Have you ever had a problem that lasted too long?

Have you ever had a problem about which you said, "I'll surely be over this by such and such a date. I'll have come out of this by then and have gone on with my life"?

Have you ever said, "By this time in my life, I surely will be married . . .

I will have had children . . .

I will have made my mark in life . . .

I will have entered fully into my ministry . . .

I will have accomplished what God created me to do"?

Problems that stay around too long are problems that drain away your life. That's what happened to this woman. She had had an issue of blood for twelve years. Her life had drained away from her.

When a problem stays around too long it isn't only the problem that grates on you, but the longevity of the problem. The problem may be the same old problem, but if it stays on and on and on, then that problem is compounded. Any time you try to confront the problem, it will whip out its résumé and remind you that you have tried that solution before, you have been to that source of help before, and it didn't work.

Your problem will begin to speak to you, "I'm here to stay forever. Nothing you can do will get rid of me. You might as well get used to me because I'm not budging. Everything you have tried has failed. Nothing is going to work. I am your problem for the rest of your life."

Your problem will remind you of a pattern of failure in your life. It will remind you of how you grew up and give you all the details of every failed relationship you have ever been in. That's because your problem has been engineered by the devil. The enemy always loves to brag about how long he has been around.

Your issue may not be of blood — in fact, it probably won't be an issue of blood. Whatever it is, however, it is like this woman's problem if it is draining the life out of you, if it's diminishing your vitality, your sparkle, your energy, your enthusiasm for living. If it isn't money, it's the children. If it isn't the children, it's the spouse. If it isn't the spouse, it's the lack of a spouse. If it isn't that, it's something else.

Your issue may be a secret in the family . . .
a secret on the job . . .

    a secret in the church . . .

        a secret from your past . . .

            a secret that involves somebody you are
            hoping will stay a secret.

Your issue today may be a need — it may be a need to touch Jesus for salvation. It may be a need to touch Him for healing in your body. It may be a need to touch Him for a restoration or reconciliation in your marriage. It may be a need to touch Him for a blessing in your family. It may be a need to touch Him for a job. It may be a need to touch Him for a miracle in your ministry.

I don't know what your issue is, but I know this: every woman has one. There's always something. Look deep enough, look long enough, listen hard enough, watch closely enough, be sensitive enough . . . and you'll discover it. You may be in denial about your own problem. Look deep into your own heart, listen to your own talk . . . you'll find it.

It is your life-draining issue that Jesus wants to heal.

185

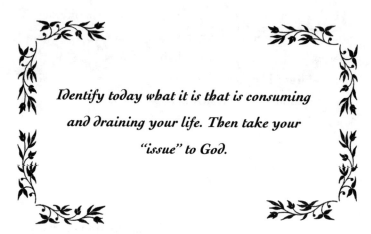

Identify today what it is that is consuming and draining your life. Then take your "issue" to God.

186

~ *Thirty-Four* ~

Own Up to Your Problem, and Take It to Jesus!

When she had

heard of Jesus,

[she] came in the

press behind . . .

— Mark 5:27

The woman with an issue of blood had experienced twelve years of hurting, pain, suffering.

While other people around her were laughing, she was in pain.

While other people around her were having a good time, she was in pain.

While other people around her were making plans, she was thinking, I'm not sure I can go on like this.

187

In any group of women you happen to be in, look around. There are women who are there in pain. They may not identify themselves. You may not be able to tell from the outside that they are suffering. But they are hurting nonetheless.

One of the main reasons women don't share their problems is this: They are told they shouldn't have problems, especially after they are saved.

Church people will say or imply, "If you were really saved, you wouldn't have this problem."

In the eleventh chapter of Hebrews, we find a list of people who are often called the heroes of the faith. On that list you'll see Noah and Abraham and Sarah and Isaac and Jacob and Joseph and Moses and Rahab and Gideon and Samson and David and Samuel and all the prophets. The amazing thing to me is that every one of these giants of faith had a problem! Problems are a part of life.

The Bible says that some of these heroes of the faith were tortured and mocked and scourged and imprisoned and stoned and sawn asunder. Now I've been cut a few times, but I have never been sawn asunder.

It says they were afflicted and tormented, and that some of them wandered in deserts and lived in caves. I've lived in some poor places, but I've never lived in a cave.

188

God's people have problems. We need to face up to that. It's not a matter of lack of faith or of not being saved. It's a matter of life in a fallen world. Problems come with the turf of a world that has been turned upside down by sin.

This woman's problem was a private problem. It was not a public problem. It was a problem that could be covered up.

Oh, we are so good at hiding our problems. Not long ago I was in a meeting where the women looked so fine, you wouldn't have thought any of them had a worry in the world. In fact, if I could have exchanged the offering at that meeting for the amount of money those women had spent on their hairdos, I gladly would have made the

exchange. They were wearing silk dresses and diamond jewelry and sequined jackets. They were looking good.

But I wasn't fooled. I knew that every imaginable secret was present in that room. That room was filled with private problems.

Various dignitaries and notable people were introduced from the platform that night. But I knew the names of many of the guests sitting out in the audience.

Sister Rape was present.

Sister Child Abuse came along.

Sister on Crack Cocaine was there.

Sister Battered Wife was there, too.

Sister Lesbian showed up.

Sister Oppressed attended.

Sister Depressed was sitting right by her side.

All the girls were present that night!

They are present in any large gathering of women anywhere in our nation at any time.

189

The fact that you have a problem is not what matters most. What matters is this: What you choose to do about your problem.

This woman made the right choice about where to take her problem.

Now, she didn't make the right choice immediately. She made it ultimately, but she didn't make it immediately.

Part of this woman's problem was that she had suffered for twelve years not only with the issue of blood but at the hand of physicians. The Bible says that she had "suffered many things of many physicians, and had spent all that she had, and was nothing bettered, but rather grew worse" (Mark 5:26).

It's one thing to have a problem and another thing to have a problem with all the people who are trying to tell you how to fix your problem. By the time she got finished with those who gave her advice, but no real help, she was worse off than she was before — because at that point she didn't have any money left!

Be careful who it is that you let treat you. That person who is so eager to treat you may just be after your money. They may just want to be able to tell others that you are their patient.

Be careful who it is that you trust to help you. That person may not be worthy of your trust.

Be careful who it is that becomes your confidant. That person may gossip about you to everybody she meets.

Beware of the counsel of the ungodly. They'll give you plenty of advice, but they can't give you any lasting help.

The ungodly counselor is not a good counselor — not about things that truly matter, not about things that affect your spirit, not about things that are eternal. David said, "Blessed is the person who walks not according to the counsel of the ungodly, nor aligns herself with sinners, nor sits in the seat of those who are scornful of the things of God." (See Psalm 1:1.)

This woman had put her trust, her faith, her hope in people who could not help her. They may have been able to describe her problem. But they had no ability to prescribe her solution.

If you are going to seek out someone to help you, seek out someone who knows the Answer. Find someone who will say to you, "Jesus is on the way. Jesus is coming. Jesus is the Healer. Jesus is the Problem-Solver. Jesus is the One who can dry up the problem that is draining you dry. Reach out and touch Him by your faith!"

Let the problem in your life hear you say, "Jesus is going to deal with you." Let the problem-causer, the enemy himself, hear you say, "Jesus is coming. And I'm not hanging around here with you any longer. I'm going to get to Him no matter what it takes."

Take your problem today to the Source of your solution. Take your problem to Jesus! Jesus has the overflow that can put a stop to your problem flow.

191

~ *Thirty-Five* ~

Yes, A Woman Like You!

Him that cometh to me I will in no wise cast out.

— John 6:37

When this unclean, bleeding woman heard that Jesus was coming, she had to come to grips with this question, "Can a woman like me touch a God like Him?"

You see . . .

The Law said that she was unclean.

The Law said that she wasn't supposed to touch anybody, much less a man, much less a rabbi.

She was considered to be lethal to a priest.

But this woman didn't pay any attention to what other people had to say about her. She refused to feel dirty about herself.

If you feel dirty about yourself, your ability to touch God is diminished — not because of anything that God has said, and not because God will reject you or deny you access to Himself. No! Your ability to touch God will be diminished because you won't reach out for Him.

The woman who feels dirty and unclean doesn't feel worthy to receive the miracle she needs. Oh, she needs the miracle alright, and she knows she needs it. But she doesn't feel worthy to receive the miracle so she doesn't pray like she needs to pray . . .

she won't praise like she needs to praise . . .

she won't worship like she needs to worship . . .

she won't reach out to seize the moment like she needs to seize the moment. A woman who feels dirty, unclean, unworthy is a woman who is going to sit on the sidelines with her problem.

When a woman has suffered from rejection, it affects the way she feels about God. She isn't sure that God will like her, that God will receive her, that God will help her.

You must reach the place where you know with certainty in your own life that God's love is for you. You must reach a place of understanding in which you say, "Yes! A woman with a past . . .

can touch a God in the present

who is able to change the future."

193

It's time to take a look at yourself and declare to the person you see in your own mirror, "It can be done."

In spite of your personal history . . .

in spite of the problem . . .

in spite of the circumstances . . .

in spite of what others say . . .

God can be touched by YOU. And He wants to be touched by you.

In spite of your heartache . . .

In spite of your pain . . .

In spite of your depression . . .

You can get to Jesus with the feelings of your infirmities. You can touch Him.

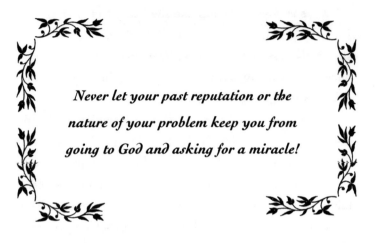

Never let your past reputation or the nature of your problem keep you from going to God and asking for a miracle!

∽ Thirty-Six ∾

Seize the
Miracle Moment

She said,

If I may touch

but his clothes,

I shall be whole.

— Mark 5:28

I like this woman with the issue of blood. She knew how to seize the moment.

We each need to learn how to seize the moment in the spirit realm. There are moments when the anointing is so strong in a meeting, you can almost cut it with a knife. It is at those times that you need to seize the moment. If you miss the moment, you may miss out on the miracle you need. There are too many things I need God to do for me to sit back in my seat when the anointing of God starts to fall. I want to jump right in. I can't afford for any of my miracles to pass me by.

195

This woman knew she was at the end of the line. She was out of health . . .

out of money . . .

out of physicians . . .

out of people who
could minister to her.

But, she wasn't out of faith.

She had run out of everything in her life but the one thing she needed. She had her belief that if she could only touch the hem of Jesus' garment, she'd be made whole.

This woman did not have any other human being helping her. Nobody was counseling her. Nobody was lobbying for her. Nobody was running interference for her. Nobody was ministering to her. She had nobody . . . she only had one person who could preach to her: herself.

Is that where you are today?

This sick, bleeding, wounded woman — weak in her body but not in her spirit — began to preach to herself. She said, "If I may but touch."

There are times when you have to encourage yourself. You can't sit and wait for somebody to rescue you. You have to get up and do what you can to rescue yourself!

She announced to the devil, "You may have caused something to be wrong with my body, but there's nothing wrong with my head. There's nothing wrong with my spirit. I know what to do. I know what to believe."

When the Bible says that she "said," the tense of that word means that she said and she said and she said. She kept on talking to herself. She told herself over and over and over again, "If I may touch but his clothes, I shall be whole."

She kept saying, "I can't die yet. I've got to touch Him. I can't give up yet. I've got to touch Him. I can't lay down and surrender yet. I've got to touch Him. And if I can't touch Him — if only I can touch His clothes — I shall be whole!"

I know people today are only alive because they are living on "If I may but touch" faith.

Touching Jesus today is all that matters.

There's nothing you can do about yesterday.

There's nothing you can do about all those lost years.

There's nothing you can do about all that wasted money.

There's nothing you can do about what people say.

There's something you can do, however, about touching Jesus.

This woman said, "I know that if I can get to Jesus, I shall be whole."

She may have had a little doubt about whether she had enough strength to get through the crowd. She may have had a question about whether she could get close enough to touch Him. She may have had some self-doubts.

But she had no doubt about Jesus. She knew that if she could get to Him, He would heal her. She believed with every ounce of her being that if she could only make contact, she would be whole.

She knew that she didn't need any other physician . . .

any other counselor . . .

any other helper . . .

any other person to minister to her . . .

if she could just get to Jesus.

Let there be no doubt in your heart today. Jesus IS the One. He IS the Healer. He IS the Savior. He IS the Deliverer.

197

Seize the opportunity that
God is giving you to touch Him!

198

~ *Thirty-Seven* ~

Press On!

[She] came in the

press behind, and

touched his garment.

— Mark 5:27

The woman with the issue of blood faced two major challenges. One was the challenge of confronting her own self-doubt, Can a woman like me touch a God like Him? The answer to that question is always "yes."

The second challenge she faced was getting through the crowd.

Once you make up your mind to get to Jesus, the devil will do everything he can to put obstacles in your way.

There's always the flesh realm that you have to break through to get to God in the spirit realm.

You have to say to those who doubt what you are doing, "Excuse me, but I'm on my way to Jesus no matter what you say."

You have to say to those who want you to stop and stroke their egos, "Excuse me, but I don't have time for your games. I'm on my way to Jesus."

You have to say to those who offer you their expert but ungodly opinions, "Excuse me, but I know where I'm going and if you'll just step out of my path, I'll be on my way."

199

Don't let anything stand in your way. Step right over everything of the flesh that the devil puts in your way and keep pushing forward to Jesus.

When justice says you can't get to Him, God's mercy lets you by.

When the Law tries to stop you, God's grace opens up a door.

When the world says, "Don't go," the Spirit of God says, "Come on!"

Our part is to press.

God's part is to make a way, to open up a path.

The enemy may be telling you that it is impossible for you to get up, get out, or get on with your life. I'm here to tell you that the devil is a liar!

This woman pressed through the crowd. She pressed through the nay-sayers and the doom-sayers.

She pressed through the doctor's report
and the pile of bills
and the laws that were
intended to shut her out.

She made her way through the crowd of
doubters
and discouragers
and the bad-news reporters.

She pressed right on through the drug dealers
on her doorstep,
the pimps on her corner,
and the gang circling her car.

She pressed through!

When this woman with an issue of blood touched Jesus, she touched His life. His life poured into every area of her body in which life had been draining away to nothing. His life filled up her lack of life.

And His life will fill up your lack of life when you touch Him today.

Press on to God today. Don't let any thing or any person stop you!

201

Part VI

Loosed to Live in the NOW

⌁ God's Baby Girl ⌁

God spoke through the prophet Ezekiel to tell His people how He regarded them — as if they were a baby girl who had been cast away upon her birth. God found her — unwanted, uncared for — in an open field, exposed to ridicule, destined to die. He called to her to live. He cared for her, washed her, salted her, and wrapped her up in swaddling clothes.

God said, however, that His baby girl hadn't been destined to remain a baby. She was intended to grow up and mature and become a mother. Just as He had nurtured her, she was to nurture others. Just as He had ministered to her, she was to minister to others. His image of her was not of her past, but of her present. He expected her to be a "woman in the now."

205

From the Scriptures:

And say, Thus saith the Lord GOD unto Jerusalem; Thy birth and thy nativity is of the land of Canaan; thy father was an Amorite, and thy mother an Hittite.

And as for thy nativity, in the day thou wast born thy navel was not cut, neither wast thou washed in water to supple thee; thou wast not salted at all, nor swaddled at all.

None eye pitied thee, to do any of these unto thee, to have compassion upon thee; but thou wast cast out in the open field, to the loathing of thy person, in the day that thou wast born.

And when I passed by thee, and saw thee polluted in thine own blood, I said unto thee when thou wast in thy blood, Live; yea, I said unto thee when thou wast in thy blood, Live.

I have caused thee to multiply as the bud of the field, and thou hast increased and waxen great, and thou art come to excellent ornaments: thy breasts are fashioned, and thine hair is grown, whereas thou wast naked and bare.

Now when I passed by thee, and looked upon thee, behold, thy time was the time of love; and I spread my skirt over thee, and covered thy nakedness: yea, I sware unto thee, and entered into a covenant with thee, saith the Lord GOD, and thou becamest mine.

— Ezekiel 16:3–8

∾ Thirty-Eight ∾

We All
Are Born "Unclean"

Except a man be

born of water and of

the Spirit, he cannot

enter into the

kingdom of God.

— John 3:5

In Ezekiel 16, the Lord likens His people to an abandoned baby girl. He says, "When I first saw you, you were a mess. You had been birthed, but you hadn't been cared for. You had been through the birth canal, but you hadn't been cleaned up." God says, "I was shocked at your neglect — the things you should have received but which you hadn't received. You were born, but you had not been washed."

207

Being a man, I didn't know very much about the birthing process before my wife became pregnant. Going into that delivery room for the first time was a trip!

I'm a veteran now. I just put on that mask and walk in there and say, "Step aside. I'm ready to deliver that baby." I don't deliver the baby, of course, but I feel ready to do it!

Before my first experience in the delivery room, the only newborn babies I had seen were ones I had seen on television. Those babies on television come out weighing about twenty pounds and they have full heads of hair. They are holding suckers and looking all around and talking to the nurses — all the time with big smiles on their faces. The babies on television all are born looking like the Gerber baby-food babies.

That was what I was expecting.

I was so shocked!

When my wife pushed out that baby I nearly screamed. I was rebuking the devil and calling for the blood to be removed and the gook to disappear. That baby didn't look at all like what I expected.

When they washed the baby, however, she started looking pretty good. I said, "Yeah, this might be alright after all."

The appearance of the baby wasn't the baby's fault. The fact is . . . she looked just like what she had been through!

The church has been trying to birth Gerber babies for centuries. But newborn babes in Christ don't look like that. They look like what they've just been through. They have just pushed their way through all kinds of mess to get to God and when they arrive in the church, they still have some of that mess clinging to them. We must not be shocked at this. Rather, we must be prepared to clean them up and care for them.

The church, by its very definition, attracts hurting people, just as a hospital attracts sick people. I recently told the congregation of my church, "Everybody in here is sick. If you're not sick, get out. Because the criteria for getting in here is that you know you are sick. Those who do not think they are sick do not feel any need for the Great Physician."

I want to be surrounded by people who know they need God. I don't have any desire at all to be around people who think that God is a theological, fanciful, abstract concept and who think it is nice to dress up and go someplace on Sunday. I want to be surrounded by those who are lame, deaf, blind, incapacitated, restricted, handicapped people who feel a need for God every hour of every day.

Jesus was attracted to hurting people. He didn't hang around the religious people who thought they were clean. He said, "You may be clean on the outside, but inside you are filthy." (See Matthew 23:25.)

At least hurting people know they are hurting. They know they are a mess when they are birthed.

Unfortunately for women, it seems the church has a special desire to see that its female babies look like Gerber babies. A double standard has developed. A man can come into the church with a long string of sins trailing behind him and the prevailing attitude is, "Well, boys will be boys. Naughty, naughty. He finally quit sowing his wild oats. Praise God." But if a woman has had two or three babies by different men and then she comes into the church and word of her past gets out, people treat her as if she has leprosy.

Pastors often make elaborate altar calls to bring in afflicted people, but once those afflicted people are saved and become a part of the church, we seem embarrassed to have them in our midst.

A shroud of secrecy is put around those who have had pasts that we are ashamed to recognize. If a woman has been scarred, raped, abused, molested, or been involved in unnatural affection, she dare not admit it.

Do you remember the woman who was taken in adultery and was brought to Jesus for Him to judge? The Bible says that the woman was caught "in the very act" of committing adultery. (See John 8:3-4.) Now if she was caught in the act, there had to have been a man there! But nobody brought him half-naked and wrapped in a blanket to a public place in the presence of the Lord. Nobody seemed ready to stone him to death although they all were eager to put her to death. The man apparently was allowed to take a shower, shave, dress himself, and crawl out the back window.

210

Do you know how horrifying it is to have other people judge your sins? Have you experienced that in your life? I know you have. We all have. People tend to be merciful toward their own sins, but when it comes to your sins, your reputation, your guilt . . . they can be ruthless.

We have placed a veil over the feminine heart in our churches. We insist that women smile and look good and say, "I'm living a victorious life in Christ." We allow them no opportunity to say, "I'm hurting. I'm wounded. I'm struggling."

When a painful issue arises in a woman's life, or in the life of her child, or in the life of her sister . . . she doesn't tell anybody. She is forced to keep a secret because no platform has been created that allows women to be real with one another without fear of being "stoned" to death. The secrets that lie untold in women's hearts are killing the church.

Can you imagine a woman coming into your church and saying during a testimony service, "I was abused as a child. I was the victim of incest and then when I got a little older I was raped. I've had four children now by three different husbands. I've had about twenty-nine boyfriends in my life and I'm presently divorced and trying hard to raise my kids. I know the Lord has saved me and here I am. I'm struggling, but I know I'm saved."

No, we expect a woman to say, "Praise God, He's with me all the time and He makes every minute of my life glorious and I thank Him for the opportunity to serve as chairman of this committee."

It's time to get real.

It's time that people heard your real testimony.

211

What drove you to the altar?

What nightmare experience drove you to fall upon His mercy and cry out to God?

Nobody cries out "Save me!" unless they are drowning.

It's time that we start looking at each other with an eye toward seeing what they've been through. It's time we see their brokenness and their heartache. It's time we see their tenacity, their ability, their faith. It's time to look inside ourselves and inside one another and to admit, "We all are born 'unclean.'"

*Take a look at someone today and see
her as God sees her. See all that has made her
who she is, and then look even deeper to see
all that God has created her to be!*

Cut the Cord

> *As for thy nativity, in the day thou wast born thy navel was not cut.*
>
> — Ezekiel 16:4

God said that when He first saw His baby girl she hadn't even had the umbilical cord cut away from her body. And that's the state for many newborn Christians. They are still tied to something in their past. They are still linked to things that they need to break away from. They are still being fed emotionally by relationships that need to be severed.

The cord to the past is cut only when a woman realizes that what she needs, she can get from a better source. We need to hold out to women the love and forgiveness and healing power of God. We need to encourage her to come to El Shaddai — the Breasted One — to receive the nurture that she needs. We need to show her how to draw from God a flow of life that will replace and nullify her need for her former life.

So often I want to tell women, "Go out and buy yourself a pair of scissors and write on it, 'Cut the cord!'" There are things you need to cut away from your life. There are relationships that you need to sever. There are habits that you need to amputate from your daily life.

213

Don't allow a guilt trip from the past strangle you or cling to you or trip you up. Cut the cord!

God wants to free you from cords of manipulation . . .
cords of blackmail . . .
cords of emotional slavery . . .
cords of bondage to someone who
seeks to control your life.

Cut the cord that ties you to the old mud holes of your past.

If a little lamb and a pig fall into the same fly-infested, dirty, oozing mud hole, the pig will wallow in the mud, but the lamb will cry to get out. It's the same mud but a different nature.

If you are a child of God and you fall in the mud, you'll start to cry, "I don't like this. I want out of this. I'm not really like this. I hate this! Help me!"

The fact that you fall into the mud or someone throws you into the mud is not the issue. What you do when you are in the mud is what matters.

Say goodbye to Joe's Bar and Ruby's Lounge.

Say goodbye to the pimp and the pusher.

Say goodbye to the drinking girls and gambling friends.

Put that addiction . . .
that abortion . . .
that sickness . . .
that divorce . . .
that failure . . .
that loss . . .
behind you!

Pronounce your own benediction on your former life. Pronounce your own last rites on your failures. Conduct your own funeral for the "old person" you were before you were saved.

Declare that the old you — the you who existed before God found you and cleaned you up and grew you up to be His woman — is dead. She doesn't exist anymore.

Declare that the old sinful patterns of your life, the old sin-producing relationships in your life are dead and gone. They don't exist for you anymore. Declare any dominating evil spirit evicted from your life. The only spirit He wants at work in your life is the Holy Spirit!

Declare that you are a new creature in Christ Jesus. The old you has died and has been buried. The new you is being resurrected!

As you cut the cord get ready for a
new enthusiasm . . .
    a new outpouring of faith . . .
        a new freshness of anointing!
God will release you to live in freedom.

215

Being born again means you are out of the womb of sin. Cut the ties that will seek to draw you back into darkness.

~ Forty ~

Washed, Salted, and Swaddled

Neither wast thou

washed in water to

supple thee;

thou wast not salted

at all, nor swaddled

at all.

— Ezekiel 16:4

The Lord was shocked that His little baby girl had not been washed. It's not the baby's responsibility to wash itself. It's not the newly saved person's responsibility to wash herself. It's our responsibility.

How should we care for a new babe in Christ?

First, we must do some washing. The Bible says we are washed by the water of His Word. (See Ephesians 5:26.) When we give the Word of God to a new babe in Christ, we wash that person. So many women have been helped by the simple application of the words of Jesus, "Woman, thou art loosed." That word of God is powerful to them; it washes something off them, out of them, and away from them.

The Word of God, spoken in mercy and by the power of the Holy Spirit, regenerates us. (See Titus 3:5.)

Second, we must do some salting. In Bible times, salt was rubbed into the skin of a newborn baby. When someone tells us today, "You have the skin of a baby," we start grinning and take it as a great compliment. Let me remind you of something you know — the skin of a newborn baby can be anything but beautiful. It can be red and chapped and bruised and peeling. Salt was applied to both heal and toughen the skin. Salting allowed the baby to be handled without bruising.

So many people need to be salted today! They are so sensitive that they can't be handled, they can't be touched, they can't be corrected or admonished. No matter what you say to them, they swell up and get defensive. They have not been salted.

When a person has been salted, she can take a licking and keep on ticking. Nobody has to call her name for her to feel good about herself. Nobody has to acknowledge her for her to know she's worthy. Nobody has to compliment her for her to feel loved.

Jesus said that those who followed Him were the salt of the earth. (See Matthew 5:13.) We get salty by our association with salt. The newborn Christian gets salty by being around salt. It is our job to accept that new believer into our midst — to make a place for her, to surround her, to include her, to allow her into our circle of friends. The way she is going to get salty is by hanging around salt!

The more a woman knows that she is accepted and loved by other women who will be honest with her and with whom she can be honest, the less she needs to be handled with kid gloves. When she feels that it's alright to be herself, she will be less defensive about hiding who she has been or who she really is on the inside.

Third, we are to do some swaddling. We each are born naked into this world but the moment we are born, we need to be covered and protected against the elements.

Some women have been exposed to too much. They've seen too much, heard too much, and experienced too much. They were too young to learn some of the things they learned. They were exposed to the hard facts of life before they could handle that exposure.

When we swaddle a newborn Christian, we are to wrap that woman up in our arms of supernatural love and say to her, "You don't need to go back to that old life that was so painful. You can start over. You can be healed of those old painful memories and start experiencing something different. You can start having good times in your life to replace those bad times. You can start having good relationships in your life to replace those bad relationships."

To swaddle a person is to give her a continual dose of God's love . . . and to give her hope for her life.

To swaddle a person is to cover her in prayer and to intercede on her behalf.

But what if you are the baby who hasn't been cared for properly?

If you are the person today who needs to be washed and there's nobody who is washing you . . .

If you are a woman who needs to be salted and there's nobody salting you . . .

If you need to be swaddled and there's no swaddling being done for you . . .

Then you need to wash, salt, and swaddle yourself!

Wash yourself by reading God's Word. Get into a church where you can hear His Word preached with Holy Ghost power. Get around people who are studying His Word and who are speaking His Word and who are living His Word.

Salt yourself by getting right into the middle of a group of godly women. Find a group of women who are living up to what Paul described as being a good setting for sound doctrine: "The aged women likewise, that they be in behavior as becometh holiness, not false accusers, not given to much wine, teachers of good things; that they may teach the young women to be sober, to love their husbands, to love their children, to be discreet, chaste, keepers at home, good, obedient to their own husbands, that the word of God be not blasphemed" (Titus 2:3–5).

Swaddle yourself by refusing to turn on that television set that fills your mind with filth and unrealistic expectations and lusts. Swaddle yourself instead with praise music and teaching tapes and videos of conferences in which God's Word is taught and God's delivering power is manifest.

219

When the devil tells you that you can't be cleaned up . . . when he tells you that you can't be salted . . .

when he tells you that you can't be swaddled . . .

look the enemy in the eye and say, "Devil, you are a liar!"

When you desire to be cleaned up, God will help you get cleaned up!

As you wash yourself, He will wash you with His forgiveness.

As you salt yourself, God will salt you with His power and presence.

As you swaddle yourself in garments of praise, God will swaddle you in His love.

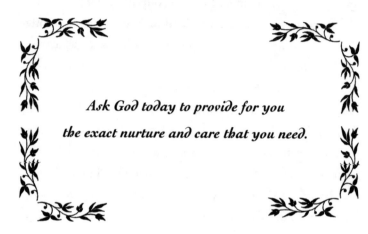

Ask God today to provide for you

the exact nurture and care that you need.

∽ Forty-One ∾

Have Compassion
on Yourself

None eye pitied thee

... to have

compassion upon

thee; but thou wast

cast out in the open

field, to the

loathing of thy

person.

— Ezekiel 16:5

God said that He was surprised at the attitude of people toward His baby girl. He said, "No one took pity on you. No one helped you."

When a woman is abused as a child, she grows up not only with the pain of that abuse, but with the anger that nobody helped her, nobody intervened on her behalf, nobody stepped in and rescued her. People may have murmured, but nobody helped.

God said, "You were cast out into the open field, and everybody loathed you." (See Ezekiel 16:5.) That's the way a woman feels if she was abused as a child. She feels as if she was a throw-away baby.

It's not only abused women who feel this way. Divorced women, rejected women, and abandoned women feel this way. In fact, virtually every woman goes

221

through this experience at some time. She feels as if she has been tossed out into an open field. She feels that nobody values or appreciates her. She feels vulnerable and despised at the same time.

There's a difference between being cast away privately and being cast away into an open public field. If someone rejects you privately, you will hurt, but you won't feel nearly as much pain as if that person rejects you or denounces you publicly. It's much more difficult to overcome the shame that attaches itself to you when you are publicly cast away.

When people reject you, it's very difficult for you to feel good about yourself. You start thinking, "Well, if they don't think I'm worth anything, I must not be worth anything. If they are willing to throw me aside, I must be of no value."

Never allow another person's actions to control how you see yourself. That's too much power to give to another human being.

If people don't have the ability to discern the inner riches of your treasure, that's their problem. But if you sit at home and wallow in self-pity because they have no discernment, that becomes your problem.

Recognize that those who reject you have no ability to see inside you. They have no ability to hear the meaning behind your words. They have no ability to feel the quality of your touch. They have bought a lie — either willfully or unconsciously — that the devil has told them about you.

Refuse to adopt their opinion of you. Because if you adopt their opinion of you, you are adopting the very opinion the devil wants you to have. He wants you to buy into the lie he has told them. Don't do it!

The fact is, if you buy that lying opinion and come to the conclusion that you don't like yourself, you can't like anybody else. If you don't treat yourself well, you won't treat others well. If you don't care for yourself, you won't care for others. We treat other people out of the well of our own self-esteem. And if your well is dry, you don't have any esteem that you can give to another person. You can't value someone else because you have no value for yourself.

The Bible says that we are to love our neighbors as we love ourselves — which means we are to love other people to the degree that we love ourselves. (See Matthew 22:39.) If we don't love ourselves, we don't have any love to give to our neighbors.

In my work as a pastor, I have counseled a number of wife-beaters. I discovered again and again that the abusing man didn't hurt his wife because he hated her. The reality was, he hated himself! He was angry at himself. He loathed himself.

The Bible says that a man is to love and nurture and care for his wife just as he loves, nurtures, and cares for his own body. (See Ephesians 5:28.) But what if he does not like his own body, his own self? How can he nurture anything inside his mate if he doesn't nurture anything inside himself? It can't be done.

People who have been treated with hate become full of hate and can only give hate.

223

People who have been criticized become filled with a critical spirit and can only give criticism.

People who have been abused become full of anger and can only give abuse.

Refuse to accept the loathing of other people. Don't allow their opinion to creep into your inner person.

Refuse to loathe yourself.

Face the reality that if no one has had compassion on you, you can still have compassion on yourself.

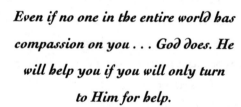

Even if no one in the entire world has compassion on you . . . God does. He will help you if you will only turn to Him for help.

224

∾ Forty-Two ∾

Live!

I said unto thee

when thou wast in

thy blood,

Live.

— Ezekiel 16:6

God said that when He found you, you were such a mess that you were in a state of emergency. In emergency situations, rules often change.

In normal situations, all vehicles stop at red lights. In a state of emergency, ambulances and police cars and fire trucks roar right through them. If you are driving to get away from a tornado that is closing in on you, a stop sign isn't going to mean anything at all to you!

225

Many of the things that God desires to do for you, He will bypass in times of emergency. He said to His baby girl, "When I found you, you were dying in your own polluted blood." (See Ezekiel 16:6.)

When He found His baby girl He found her covered with blood, bruised and raw, naked, and strangling on the cord of her birth. She was lying out in an open field, cast away by everybody, dying!

When God found you, you were in a deplorable state, too. I don't know the circumstances of your life or what it is that drove you to the altar to accept Jesus as your Savior, but I know it was something deplorable. I know you were dying. You had been polluted by life, strangled by sin, bruised and raw because of the treatment of other people. Your past made you naked and exposed. You were cast away in loathing.

There was no time for God to tell you all that He wanted to say to you. He had only one word to speak to all of your abuse . . .

all of your trauma . . .

all of your trials . . .

all of your tears . . .

all of your pain . . .

all of your addictions.

God had only one word to speak to you in answer to your depression, your thoughts of suicide, your feelings of unworthiness.

There was no time for Him to teach you Hebrew or Greek or to define for you redemption, substitution, election, predestination, justification, or sanctification. In your state of emergency there was only one word God could speak to you that would matter.

He said to you, "LIVE!"

And that's the foremost word we each need to speak to those who are suffering or who are in pain today. It's the word we each need to hear when we feel the raw bruising pain of rejection and isolation and abuse. The word is "LIVE!"

To the woman who has just been told that she is going to be divorced, God says, "LIVE!"

To the woman who has just been beaten to a pulp by her husband, God says, "LIVE!"

To the woman who has just buried her infant child or her beloved husband of forty years, God says, "LIVE!"

To the woman who has just been raped, God says, "LIVE!"

To the woman who has just been fired from her job, God says, "LIVE!"

To the woman who is overwhelmed right now by her past, her outer problems, or her inner pain, God says, "LIVE!"

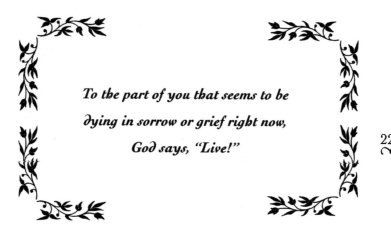

To the part of you that seems to be dying in sorrow or grief right now, God says, "Live!"

227

✍ Forty-Three ✍

Move From the Past to NOW

Beloved,

now are we

the sons of God.

— 1 John 3:2

God said to the orphaned girl that He had rescued, helped, and raised, "Now when I see you, I see what you have become." (See Ezekiel 16:8.) God knew all along that His baby girl was going to become a woman. He expected it to happen. He helped it to happen. And it did. He says, "Now when I see you, I don't see you as you were. I see you only as you are."

Focus on that word *now*.

People often talk about a woman being "in the know." I like to talk about a woman being "in the now."

There comes a time when you have to draw a line between then and now.

There comes a time when you must say, "That was then. Now is now. I used to do that. Now I do this. I used to be that. Now I am this."

Part of your maturity — part of your growing up to be God's woman — is to draw a line between the unwashed, unsalted, unswaddled, cord-bound baby that you were, and the mature, ornamented, breasted woman in Christ that you are."

There will come a time when you must declare that the crisis in your life is over.

You didn't die.

You didn't lose your mind.

You didn't fall off the end of the earth.

You didn't crumble into a heap.

You are alive. You are strong. You made it. You are a survivor of whatever it was that the devil tried to do to you to keep you from God's salvation and take you out of God's plan.

There will come a time when you must get rid of the rotting, decaying, dead bodies that you have been carrying around. Some women have been carrying around old relationships and old experiences so long that they've become accustomed to the stench of them. God declares that thing to be dead in your life. It's time for you to bury it so you can get on with the resurrection He has planned for you.

229

Make a decision today to bury anything that has pulled you down, held you back, kept you in despair, limited you, deceived you, or made you vulnerable. Throw it into the coffin. Lower it into the ground. Declare it over in your life.

Everything you can't change and can't fix . . .

Every childhood trauma . . .

Every secret disgrace . . .

Every memory of abuse . . .

Every instance of rejection . . .

Every addiction . . .

Every fear . . .

Every failure . . .

Must be buried in Christ Jesus! Commit those things to the Lord once and for all. Give them to Him. Seal them up in a grave forever. And rise up.

You have been cleaned up . . .

freed . . .

salted . . .

clothed . . .

loved . . .

and raised to

maturity in Christ.

It's time for you to experience His resurrection power and live in the now.

Draw a line between who you were and what you are — and step over into the NOW!

~ *Forty-Four* ~

The Process
of Wholeness

... Unto the

measure of the

stature of

the fulness

of Christ.

— Ephesians 4:13

Birth and growth are two different processes, both naturally and spiritually. There's a difference between being saved and being healed until you are whole. Salvation happens instantly. Healing can be a lifelong process.

When God saves you, He quickens the eternal part of you. He calls it to come to life and it springs to life in a moment of time. Your spirit is immediately changed by the Holy Ghost and you can never be any more saved than you are in that moment.

231
~

If you compare a person who just died with a person who died twenty years ago, there's no difference in their state of "deadness." They are equally dead. The same principle holds for your salvation. You are either saved or you aren't. It's a state of being, not a state of becoming. If you were made alive in Christ, then you are alive in Christ.

When you were saved, God gave you everlasting life and illumined your innermost being with an eternal light. Your salvation was a supernatural impartation of God in your most secret place — your spirit.

Even though your spirit has been saved, you can still have some areas in your mind, your emotions, your appetites, and your desires that need to be healed.

In every one of us, there is something that needs to be healed. And until it is healed, you will continue to fall back into the same cesspool of sinful behavior again and again and again.

There are those who will tell you, "If you were really saved, you wouldn't act like that. You wouldn't want to do that. You wouldn't sin like that." Lapses into error have nothing to do with the salvation of your spirit. They have to do with the healing of your soul and the fact that you are not yet whole.

There are also those who say, "Well, if she knew it was wrong, she wouldn't do it, but she doesn't know any better." No . . . you can know what is right to do and still struggle with doing it.

A preacher friend of mine once said, "It's not enough to preach against sin, because sin is not the real issue. Sin is not the problem. Sin is merely how a person seeks to medicate their problem."

In other words, whatever sin seems to plague you the most, that sin has become your method for medicating your inner pain. And the reason a person keeps sinning after they are saved is because they are still hurting.

We preachers tend to offer seminars and conferences and classes and counseling sessions that tell people to stop sinning and to start living right. The people who attend those meetings try . . . and then fail. So we teach again, and they try again . . . and fail again. So we teach some more, and they try some more . . . and fail some more. Why? Because we never get down to the real problems. We never get down to the real void. We never get down into the mouth of the lion.

Sin is how we medicate the need we have for validation. It's how we numb our pain.

We go to the marketplace seeking to buy intimacy and we end up coming home with only sexuality. You can have sexuality without having intimacy. And when that happens, there's guilt, there's shame, there's disappointment. The need for intimacy remains — in fact, it grows. And all the while, the secret need for intimacy never finds expression and is never cured.

We go to the marketplace seeking to buy peace and we come home with a fifth of alcohol. You can have numbed senses without having peace. And when that happens, there's guilt and shame and frustration and disappointment in the aftermath of your getting sober. The need for peace remains — yes, it grows. And all the while, your secret need for peace lurks in your soul and is never really addressed.

It doesn't make any difference how much money you make, or where you live, or how big your house is, or how cute you are.

233

You can be suicidal as you drive your Mercedes down the street.

You can be depressed as you sit in your big house.

You can be depressed whether you are married or single.

Your answer does not lie in people or in things. It lies in the presence of God.

Wholeness comes when you turn to Him in your weakness, your pain, your suffering, and you allow Him to do for you what no one else can do.

Only God can regenerate the human spirit. And only God can raise a person to spiritual maturity and wholeness.

Trust God today to FINISH the good work He has started in you.

∾ Forty-Five ∾

Raised to Maturity for the Purpose of Ministry

Freely ye

have received,

freely give.

— Matthew 10:8

God said to His grown-up girl, "I caused you to multiply as the bud of the field and to increase and to become great. I have given you ornaments so that you are attractive to other people. I have caused you to grow to maturity." (See Ezekiel 16:7.)

The Bible paints a very graphic picture of the little girl who has now grown up because of God's care. She has breasts. She has passed through puberty into adulthood. She now has the capacity to bear children and nurse them.

That's what God desires for every woman who comes to Him as a newborn baby Christian. He wants to raise her up so that she can birth spiritual children and then nurture those spiritual babies so that they grow up in Christ. He wants to prepare her to give to others of her love, not her anger, pain, or bitterness. He wants to mature her so that she can say to others, "The God who rescued me and delivered me and gave me life and raised me up is the same God who can and will do all that for you."

God wants to raise up women who will declare:

"The same God who brought me through can bring you through."

"The same God who helped me can help you."

"The same God who saved me can save you."

"The same God who is healing me can heal you."

God wants His women to have milk so they can nurse and nurture spiritual sons and daughters.

I believe that if you ask Him, God will show you why you had to go through what you went through so you would be who you are right now.

I believe that if you desire for Him to tell you, God will reveal to you all that He still has to give to you and all that He wants for you to do in ministry to others.

Now that He has brought you through the crisis and raised you up to maturity, you are ready to enter into the fullness of His destiny for you.

236

All the while that He was cleaning you up and cutting away from your life what needed to be cut away, He was preparing for you the blessings that He now wants you to receive.

He brought you to the bloody cross and through the cold tomb of death, and now He is ready for you to enter into the glory of resurrection time.

Your eyes have not yet seen and your ears have not yet heard and neither has it entered into your heart all the things that God has prepared for you! NOW is the time to see, to hear, and to believe. NOW is the time for blessing.

Believe God today for His NOW
blessing in your life. Ask Him to reveal
to you how you might help and
bless others. NOW is your time
to enter into His service — no longer
as His orphaned baby girl, but as His
woman. He has loosed you so that you
might loose others in His name.

237

ABOUT THE AUTHOR
Bishop T.D. Jakes

T.D. Jakes is the senior pastor and founder of The Potter's House church in Dallas, Texas. His national broadcast has been widely viewed in millions of homes across the nation. His message transcends social and gender barriers with its deep, healing wisdom and restoration for God's people. Bishop Jakes frequently ministers in massive crusades and conferences. In addition to these responsibilities, he is a highly celebrated author with several bestselling books to his credit.

To contact T.D. Jakes write:

T.D. Jakes Ministries
P.O. Box 210887
Dallas, Texas 75211

Additional copies of this book and other book titles
from ALBURY PUBLISHING are
available at your local bookstore.

Albury Publishing
P.O. Box 470406
Tulsa, Oklahoma 74147-0406

In Canada books are available from:
Word Alive
P.O. Box 670
Niverville, Manitoba
CANADA ROA 1EO

DEVOTION NOTES

DEVOTION NOTES

Devotion Notes

DEVOTION NOTES

DEVOTION NOTES

DEVOTION NOTES

DEVOTION NOTES

DEVOTION NOTES

DEVOTION NOTES